A CATHOLIC HANDBOOK ON *Sex*

ESSENTIALS FOR THE 21ST CENTURY
Explanations, Definitions, Prompts, Prayers, and Examples

WILLIAM C. GRAHAM

Paulist Press
New York / Mahwah, NJ

Nihil obstat
Rev. Msgr. James M. Cafone
February 3, 2011

Imprimatur
Most Rev. John J. Myers, D.D., J.C.D., Archbishop of Newark
March 8, 2011

Cover and book design by Lynn Else

Library of Congress Cataloging-in-Publication Data

Graham, William C., 1950–
    A Catholic handbook on sex : essentials for the 21st century : explanations, definitions, prompts, prayers, and examples / William C. Graham.
        p. cm.
    ISBN 978-0-8091-4737-3 (alk. paper)
    1. Sex—Religious aspects—Catholic Church—Miscellanea. 2. Catholic youth—Sexual behavior—Miscellanea. 3. Catholic Church—Doctrines—Miscellanea. I. Title.
    BX1795.S48G74 2011
    261.8'3570835—dc23
                                                                2011018465

Published by Paulist Press
997 Macarthur Boulevard
Mahwah, New Jersey 07430

www.paulistpress.com

Printed and bound in the
United States of America

God created man in his image;
in the divine image he created him;
male and female he created them.

God blessed them, saying:
"Be fertile and multiply; fill the earth and subdue it.
Have dominion over the fish of the sea, the birds
    of the air,
and all the living things that move on the earth."
God also said: "See, I give you every seed-bearing
    plant
all over the earth and every tree
that has seed-bearing fruit on it to be your food;
and to all the animals of the land,
all the birds of the air, and all the living creatures
that crawl on the ground,
I give all the green plants for food."
And so it happened.
God looked at everything he had made,
and he found it very good.

• Genesis 1:26–31

What has been is what will be,
and what has been done is what will be done;
and there is nothing new under the sun.
• Ecclesiastes 1:9

And the One who sat upon the throne said,
"Behold, I make all things new."
• Revelation 21:5

Christian, remember your dignity.
• Pope St. Leo the Great

You have a ton of worms in that can.
• Anthony Barrett

CONTENTS

ACKNOWLEDGMENTS

I am grateful to all who, in any way and many ways, have contributed to getting this little book into print:

Paul McMahon, the then managing editor of Paulist Press, first suggested the idea of *A Catholic Handbook on Sex* and encouraged me each step of the way; Dr. Nancy de Flon, also of Paulist Press, was part of the process early on, and carefully edited the final copy with attentiveness, efficiency, and grace.

Students at the College of St. Scholastica in Duluth, Minnesota, by their perceptive queries and comments, helped shape both questions and answers; Nick Stauber, Ben Grieger, Jon Koch, and Aleksis Kincaid were helpful in asking or refining questions and in conversation; students in my God for Guys class and in my sacraments seminar in the spring semester of 2010 were eager to be helpful not just with thoughtful comments but also with occasionally rolled eyeballs. I admire and am grateful for their patience with me. Nick was the first and very careful reader of the complete text. As a promising writer himself, he was an especially attentive editor, confidently noting with red ink in the margins what he has sometimes seen in the margins of his own graded papers. And he made me laugh with a number of his comments: "This is a long sentence; just saying." "I

had to look this word up." "Repetitive." "Awk[ward]." Dr.
Anthony Barrett reviewed the questions and was helpfully
provocative. I am grateful to the College of St. Scholastica
for granting me a sabbatical in 2011 to bring this manu-
script to completion.

Help and challenge are never far away: Tony Orman
asked me a question and made a wry comment in Ace
Hardware one April afternoon that I went right home to
write down. Molly Keating, my coauthor of *The Catholic
Wedding Book* (Paulist, 1988 and 2008), was helpful with
questions and critiques, and she exercised a firm editorial
hand as the chapter on prayer took shape. Dr. Lee Stuart
demonstrated that the conversation is never complete by
sending me another dozen questions when I thought I had
finished and kept them coming even after that. So also did
Fr. Timothy Backous, OSB, with whom I collaborated on
*Common Good, Uncommon Issues: A Primer in Moral
Theology* (Liturgical Press, 1997), which, by the way, he
and I both recommend to readers of these pages.

Unless otherwise noted, the Bible translation used here
is the New American Bible. Quotations from and references
to the *Sacramentary* will be found in the edition of Paul VI.[1]

To all who assisted, I am happy to offer thanks.
However, any shortcomings in this text are my responsibility alone.

> *William C. Graham*
> *On the shore of Spike's Lake in Minnesota*
> *May 1, 2010*

---

1. *The Roman Missal, Revised by Decree of the Second Vatican Ecumenical Council
and Published by Authority of Pope Paul VI*, 1974.

AN INTRODUCTION

Any Catholic consideration of human sexuality must begin with God's creation of man and woman "in our image, after our likeness" (Gen 1:26). And remember, "God looked at everything he had made, and he found it very good" (1:31). So any consideration that does not begin with goodness and with grace is somehow suspect.

Similarly, any question about human sexuality that begins, "How bad would it be if…" is also suspect. Sex and sexuality are gifts of God. Our use of these gifts ought to distinguish us as Catholics, so we can continue to pray in hope-filled confidence to the One to whom we give thanks: "See and love in us / what you see and love in your Son" (Preface for Sundays in Ordinary Time VII). A Catholic understanding of human sexuality and the employment of our sexual powers ought to help us become like God, so that we "come to share in the divinity of Christ, who humbled himself to share in our humanity" (the prayer of the priest as water is added to the wine at the preparation of the gifts).

We are the people "freed from sin and death / and called to the glory that has made us / a chosen race, a royal priesthood, / a holy nation, a people set apart." We are called, we say in prayer to God, to proclaim "your mighty works / for you have called us out of darkness / into your

1

own wonderful light" (Preface for Sundays in Ordinary Time I).

Called from darkness, children of the Light know that human sexuality is not just about the pleasures of the flesh, but about the witness of holy lives. And holy lives need be neither dull nor lacking in pleasure. So our questions are not about "What and how much can I get away with and still hope to see the face of God?" Rather, we ask, "How can I feel confident that my deeds and my attitudes are in keeping with human dignity so that I can act and walk confidently as a son or daughter of the Most High God?"

So what does the Church teach? How did it arrive at such an approach? If I do not immediately understand the wisdom of a position or teaching, shall I presume that the Church is wrong and should change to share my opinion? What if I find some teachings difficult? What if they are not particularly difficult to understand, but just hard to put into practice? These are the questions that will launch our considerations here, faithful both to Church teaching and also to what it means to be a human person. St. Irenaeus of Lyons, an early Church father and doctor of the Church, writing in the last quarter of the second century in what is now France, noted, "The glory of God is [wo]man fully alive."[2]

Those who seek only a good time will find this book out of step with that desire. Those who seek to participate as fully as possible in what it means to be both fully human and fully alive will, I hope, be both cheered and challenged here.

I hope, too, that these questions will prompt further discussion and more questions. I invite readers who wish to

---

2. From *Against Heresies*, written about AD 185 (Lib. 4, 20, 5–7; SC 100, 640–42, 644–48).

continue the dialogue to send along questions that could be gathered into a future volume. Questions with CATHOLIC SEX HANDBOOK in the subject line can be sent to me at WCGNYCPL@aol.com.

Unlike *A Catholic Handbook*, which has endnotes, *A Catholic Handbook on Sex* has footnotes. I like footnotes.[3] But more important, the students who were among the first readers of the previous volume said without apology that they agreed with their classmate Nicole, who pronounced, "Probably the endnotes are good. But I'll never see 'em."

Now let the quest continue so that we can participate in the divine mystery and enjoy the goodness of God!

---

3. And those in this text, I think, contain some important and interesting information!

BEFORE HEADING OFF

At the beginning of this book, you quote your colleague Dr. Anthony Barrett as saying, "You have a ton of worms in that can." What can? Worms? What do you mean?

The questions that follow suggest that we have many issues and concerns about what it means to be human and how humans can exercise their sexuality in ways that will promote wholeness and prompt holiness as they seek God while seeking to avoid harm, degradation, and sin. This, it seems, is part of what Jesus meant when he said, "I came so that they might have life and have it more abundantly" (John 10:10).

But whenever issues touch our lives in a way that can provoke heated dialogue and misunderstanding—or differing opinions, outlooks, and judgments—people are sure to be provoked. And when the topic is sex or sexuality, the uproar can be thunderous, bordering on cacophony and leading to deafness or sensory overload. There are many hot topics considered here, and how the Church approaches them is not always how individuals choose to approach them. Tony is quite correct: the sorting out of the mess that could ensue from attending to all these provocative questions is both can and worms, a ton of them.

A quick look at the questions you intend to address points to lots of controversy, but what do they all have to do with being Catholic? And is there some theology here?

Whenever we seek to conform our lives to the Gospel's commands and invitations, whenever we seek to make our hearts like the heart of Jesus, we are doing theology. In the twelfth century, St. Anselm described theology as "faith seeking understanding."[4] So our seeking is part of the theological enterprise.

Belonging to a Church is a public statement that my own thought or opinion is not the last word. The goal of this book is to help us shape our opinions, judgments, and life journey by the example of Jesus and the reflections and teachings of the Church. Those who are certain that what they thought as they got out of bed this morning is as good as it gets will find this book's Catholic approach either annoying or challenging. I am hoping for challenging.

Here's what I don't get: Why is a priest writing a book on sex? Shouldn't you guys be getting ready for Mass, or saying your prayers, or doing something holy? Shouldn't someone who is young like me, but has some experience, write about sex? No offense.

None taken. There may be books by randy teenagers or sexually experienced collegians on the market, though I have not seen them. But participating in sexual activity is no guarantee that the participant can explain what the Church teaches or even what it's all about. The reflections here begin with what the Church teaches; they invite you to con-

---

4. St. Anselm, *Proslogium*, Preface.

sider your own attitudes and actions in that light. Let me know how that works out for you.

But what about the tone of your questions? Some of them seem, well, irreverent or even flip. While your answers seem like faithful, orthodox explanations of what the Church teaches, aren't you worried that the questions may cause readers to stop reading? And who's asking these questions?

The questions that follow in these pages are real and either have been asked of me or could have been asked. They were asked in the classroom, college hallways, my office and living room, the chapel gathering space, parish churches, sacristies and vestibules, a Bally's gym, this afternoon in Ace Hardware, over the phone, and by e-mail. The questions reflect the hope, the angst, the suffering, and the concerns of the people of God who really do seek to understand. You'll see the names of some of these questioners in the acknowledgments at the front of the book, though some are not listed because they may not wish to be associated in print with queries that could sound scurrilous.

Every age and group has concerns about sex and sexuality. You will note that questions seem to be posed by both males and females, by parents, by adults, and by younger people. Some few of the questions are posed by victims of abuse. The questions may make us cringe; perhaps they should. Sometimes cringing can bring on virtue. I hope that pious eyes are not offended by the inclusion of queries from those who ask without oodles of tact. Not everyone who is alienated or angry wants to remain alienated or angry. If we take their queries at face value and give serious, thoughtful answers, perhaps they will feel the "Welcome home" that we wish to extend.

College students can be[5] colorful, provocative, and even sometimes almost offensive in what they ask or how they ask. Wounded or confused, sometimes bored, they may mean to be offensive: "Well, the Church clearly teaches," they begin, and then invent an almost impossibly hateful premise. An angry rebuttal might please them. But, "I am not familiar with that particular teaching; perhaps you can tell me more about it" may begin a dialogue. These questions and the questioners, while they may sometimes seem over the top or even hostile, really do beg to be taken seriously and can offer the opportunity to show the wisdom of a teaching that has never been encountered or considered, much less understood.

I firmly believe that questions asked in what appears to be irreverence are often an invitation to teach reverence. And human hearts are by nature more inclined to reverence than to irreverence. For all the reasons listed here, and out of respect for the questioners and their very real quests, I have resisted calls to sanitize the questions. Further, I am grateful to all the questioners; they have offered an opportunity to reconsider the Gospel anew in this effort to evangelize.

I want to suggest that a variety of folks are the targeted audience. Don't let the questions themselves put you off, because even when the questioners seem abrasive, they are seeking the truth. Do consider the answers with the idea that we are invited to test our opinions and our attitudes,

---

5. I am in midsentence, writing as I listen to a guest lecturer who is really quite boring. A student just asked him a question using a four-letter, barnyard word that would have caused a mom in the last generation to wash out such a mouth with a bar of Lava. Not one of the thirty students and professors present seemed even to notice or react to his, umm, colorful vocabulary. Times change and sometimes, sadly, we and our folkways and *mores* with them.

and even our question-asking techniques, against the teachings of the Church. The goal is to conform our hearts to the heart of Jesus because "your light must shine before others, that they may see your good deeds and glorify your heavenly Father" (Matt 5:16).

We all kind of know, sort of, what the Church teaches, right?

Many people are under the impression that they have a firm grasp on all that the Church teaches when, in fact, their information often comes from *Time* magazine or *The Wall Street Journal*, other news reports, a FOX News commentator, or people who pass on what they think they may have learned in Sunday school back in the day. There are many good and faithful Catholic people, attentive to the Church's life of prayer and community, whose understanding of the faith is not at the level of their understanding of their own professions or other interests.

Many folks who were baptized but not catechized somehow consider themselves expert on what the Church teaches. Others think they learned it all in six years in a Catholic school. When asked, "Are you a scientist after those six years because you studied science, too?" they look surprised. But how can they be theologians or masters of religious practice with no real training or education?

None of us knows as much as we might, because seeking the truth is a lifelong task. In an e-mail dialogue, an especially perceptive student noted, "I would humbly proffer to you these two patterns in your arguments regarding those who have negative feelings regarding religion. First, you point out that they are lacking information, and therefore do not have enough academic knowledge to make an informed opinion. Second, you rely on the idea that the knowledge of a group is more than the sum of its individuals, and that a group can more accurately guide individuals." Aleksis gets an A.

Can you set out a Catholic theology of sex that would set the context for what follows: a theology that considers the topic in terms of the concept of the human being? Should this include dignity—humanity made in God's image and worthy of respect?

Easy. Sex is one of God's gifts and is therefore good, just as we are good because we are made by God in the divine image. But like all good gifts, life and sex can be used either as tools or as weapons. Not every use of a good gift is good. But all the Church's teachings through all the ages and in every place invite us, as faithful stewards, to use all gifts well. We cannot use them well if we merely seek pleasure without a consideration of consequences and responsibility. We cannot truly consider consequences or responsibility, or claim that we seek either true love or true justice, if we are not well aware of our human dignity at every step and juncture. And even when others may debase themselves, we do not have the freedom to disrespect or disregard their dignity: they, using free will, may squander their dignity; we are still bound to respect it and them while we speak the truth with love (Eph 4:15, 25). In this way, we seek to be fully human and to give glory to God. When our lives are used or our sexuality is employed in any other way, we are called to make a critical examination of our days and our deeds.

Doesn't the ongoing sexual-abuse crisis prove that the Church has nothing to say about sex and sexual activity that would profit us?

The worldwide sexual-abuse crisis is a sad chapter in the Church's history. We cannot explain it away. Together with the victims and those who have failed us by their sins and inattentiveness to duty, all of us must endure in hope. Pope Benedict XVI has called all the Church to do penance and to continue to commit to a firm purpose of amendment. We should be aware, however, that the presence of criminal activity and sinfulness in our midst does not cancel the wisdom that the Church brings to all our deliberations, or the holiness of all the countless good women and men who seek to live the Gospel tradition in faithfulness and grace.

What you say sounds good. What the Church says does not. Why won't the Church listen to you?

Priests and other Church teachers often hear this comment, meant probably to be a compliment, when we explain a Church teaching, seek to put it into context, or show how it can have a positive impact on our deliberations and our lives. The teachings in this book are not my ideas or opinions, but are rather faithful, orthodox explanations of what the Church teaches.

Can one really suggest that the Church's approach to sex somehow relates to a quest for justice?

Every single utterance of the Church on sexual matters begins with or grows out of an absolute commitment to human dignity. There can be no real concern for justice without such a commitment. So the Church's approach to sex is rooted in its commitment to justice for every person and in every situation.

Isn't religion just all about rules? And aren't those rules arbitrary and meaningless?

Some folks have the idea that religion is all about rules. But really, it is all about seeking both guidance and companionship in finding, embracing, and following the Way. Religion is not a solitary effort, but calls together a community of seekers, because the human quest for meaning is never undertaken in isolation. It is in community that life's meaning and values are communicated. To have remote authority figures imposing laws or restrictions that are arbitrary and meaningless would impede the true search.

Jesus says, "Enter through the narrow gate; for the gate is wide and the road broad that leads to destruction, and those who enter through it are many. How narrow the gate and constricted the road that leads to life. And those who find it are few" (Matt 7:13–14). Seeking goodness is more difficult than being discovered by evil.

Who was Jacques Maritain, and what did he mean when he said, "Sainthood is not the negation of human life"? I thought sainthood meant giving up everything, and being both poor and miserable until you get to heaven.

Maritain was a French Catholic philosopher who died in 1973. His statement seems to suggest that being a saint is about living richly in the presence of grace, not about seeking deprivation. In her book *On Pilgrimage*, the Catholic Worker cofounder Dorothy Day advises that we must cultivate divine life. She points to the Scripture verse, "Whether you eat or whether you drink, do all for the glory of God [1 Cor 10:31]." She concludes, "This does not mean that we do not enjoy our spaghetti for lunch. God gives us natural happiness too, in order to help us love him."

We who live in the embrace of the Communion of Saints are called to make our every thought, word, and deed opportunities to embrace goodness. Surely this idea is a model for how we should view our human sexuality, and a guide for us in employing our sexual powers.

Henry David Thoreau, in the nineteenth century, had his eye on the rich reward of properly undertaken exploration when he observed in the Conclusion to *Walden* that "it is not worth the while to go round the world to count the cats in Zanzibar." Are you inviting us to count cats or take a trip to Zanzibar, or do you have something more substantial in mind here?

Thoreau insists that the most valuable travel does not require departure from home; it is the inward voyage of soul-searching. The ancient Greeks advised, "Know thyself." The Christian twist on this exploration is to invite us to inform our consciences and then examine them daily. That's substantial.

What should we know about a Catholic view of conscience before beginning?

The Second Vatican Council taught that in our consciences we discover a law that we have not invented but must obey. This voice calls us to love, to do what is good, and to avoid evil. This call is a law inscribed in the heart by God, and our dignity lies in observing it.

The conscience is our secret core where we are alone with God, whose voice echoes within. By being loyal to the call of conscience, Christians are joined to all other people of good will in the search for truth and for correct solutions to moral problems that are both personal and social in nature.[6]

We need to educate ourselves and others as together we seek to become better persons and to build a better world. Not only must we individually seek to do good and avoid evil, we must also attend to the structures and systems in society so that together we can build a better, more-just social order. This is a tall order not just for our individual lives but also for the world in which we live.

St. Paul helps us to understand our call when he writes: "Have among yourselves the same attitude that is also yours in Christ Jesus, Who, though he was in the form of God, / did not regard equality with God something to be grasped" (Phil 2:5–6).

Is it not enough simply to ask, "What would Jesus do?"

It would not be enough. In recent years, we have seen bracelets, hats, sweatshirts, and jewelry emblazoned with "WWJD." And most of those people who wonder "What Would Jesus Do?" have heard, at least once, "Jesus certainly would not spend $24.95 on that baseball hat!"

Consider this example: A cable car now runs up the mountain from the ancient town of Jericho, enabling both tourists and pilgrims to ascend in five minutes rather than hike, as Jesus did, for half an hour or more in the heat of the

---

6. See *Gaudium et spes* 16: http://www.vatican.va/archive/hist_councils/ii_vatican_council/documents/vat-ii_cons_19651207_gaudium-et-spes_en.html.

day. A report on National Public Radio some years ago featured complaints from some of the few Orthodox monks of the Monastery of the Temptation (built on the spot where local piety says Jesus was tempted by Satan), who insist that pilgrims should trek up on foot as Jesus did. Their assertion is contradicted by the developer who claims that Jesus, were he alive today (!), would definitely ride.

What would Jesus do? Would he make spiritual choices much like my own, or would he choose the option that best supports your commercial interests? (If we do not agree, well, perhaps we need an ancillary Jesus.)

What would Jesus drive? Who would he take to the prom? Who would he vote for? Perhaps rather than ask what Jesus might do should he find himself in a situation identical to my own (as if the Redeemer of all humankind had nothing better to do at the right hand of the Father in glory), we might more profitably seek to discover how to make our hearts like the heart of Jesus: compassionate, forgiving, generous, and grace filled. While it sounds certain and holy, suggesting that my choice is Jesus' choice, or vice versa, is in fact dangerous. Who decides what to do when we disagree about what Jesus would do? Those who do not agree about what Jesus would do seem to offer latter-day affirmation of an observation by Walter Rauschenbusch, the chief prophet of the American Social Gospel movement in the first part of the twentieth century: "The disciples cannot keep pace with the sweep of the Master. They flutter where he soared. They coarsen and materialize his dreams."[7]

With our eyes fixed on Jesus and the choices he made, we hope that our own choices are also faithful to what it means to be seeking fullness of life. Church teachings help

---

7. Walter Rauschenbusch, *Christianity and the Social Crisis* (New York: Macmillan & Co., 1907), 93.

us find the way to the Way, that we might craft hearts like the heart of Jesus, provoking in us deeper and more fruitful considerations about God's reign and the call to each member of the Body of Christ to be perfected "as your heavenly Father is perfect" (Matt 5:48). Seeking perfection is more difficult than tripping over "good enough" or "not so bad." Holier and, in the end, more rewarding too.

I

SEX AND THE BIBLE
IN THE BEGINNING

Does the Book of Genesis start us thinking about sex right away?

Yes. Genesis has hardly begun the story of earth's creation when we read, "God made all kinds of wild animals, all kinds of cattle, and all kinds of creeping things of the earth. God saw how good it was" (1:25). The good God was clearly fond of the good creation, and in the next verse he makes man and woman. God then surveyed all of creation, "and he found it very good" (1:31). Note, too, that when God blesses the man and woman, he says, "Be fertile and multiply" (1:26). So, not only were sex and sexuality there from the very beginning, but they also began with and are always linked to God.

Does Genesis give good guidance?

Yes. When God first creates the man and the woman, he says, "Let them have dominion over the fish of the sea, the birds of the air, and the cattle, and over all the wild animals and all the creatures that crawl on the ground" (1:26). This does not mean to wreck the earth if that seems like it would be a good day for you, but rather to be good and

17

faithful stewards. Know that all of creation is sacred; everything and everyone has a place. The message is clear: work to make it work. When we do not do that, the earth is in trouble. So are we. It took quite a while, many centuries in fact, to figure that out. But Genesis seems to have had it figured out for us long, long ago. We must not have been reading carefully, or our reading comprehension was low. Or, reading the Bible may not be as easy as we sometimes think.

God also recognized the human need for companionship: "It is not good for the man to be alone. I will make a suitable partner for him" (2:18). This, clearly, is important.

Did Genesis really lay the foundation for the idea of marriage?

Yes. In God's decree that it is not good to be alone, and in the command to be fertile and multiply, we see the basis for what we have come to understand as marriage. And marriage thus has two divinely instituted purposes: the love shared by the man and woman who become husband and wife, and the ongoing population of the earth.

How did we get from the Old Testament approach of "as many wives and concubines as a man could afford" to "one man–one woman"?

There is much in the Old Testament that is puzzling even to scholars—multiple wives and concubines among the puzzlements. But one of the most positive contributions of the Church to all of civilization has been the practice of holding all men and women to the same ethic: marriage requires the consent of both the man and the woman (thus, a woman cannot be given to a man for marriage by her father or male relative), and a man may have just one wife, and a wife just one husband. This was a gradual development over the course of the centuries, and surely reflects a high respect for the human dignity of both men and women and for their free will in entering marriage.

If sex is good, what's up with all the "Thou shall not's"?

In Exodus 20, and again in Deuteronomy 5, we find the Ethical Decalogue, or the Ten Commandments. The statements are imperative, telling us what to do and not to do both in our relationship to God and in social relationships as well. The Commandments remind us that there are no neutral actions: what we do and how we act either makes us better or stronger in response to God's grace, or distresses or weakens us as we choose something other than the fullness of life. Those concerned by the "you shall not" in the following command can recast it positively and consider the exercise time well spent with Scripture: "You shall not covet your neighbor's house. You shall not covet your neighbor's wife, nor his male or female slave, nor his ox or ass, nor anything else that belongs to him" (Exod 20:17). Remember to make it inclusive of both genders as well.

When Lot's wife turned to a pillar of salt, was that all about sex? And does that mean that salt is bad?

In Genesis 19, we read that "the LORD rained down sulphurous fire upon Sodom and Gomorrah (from the LORD out of heaven)" (19:24). Ruined their day. Lot and his family had been instructed, "Flee for your life! Don't look back or stop" (19:17). But, speaking of ruined days, "Lot's wife looked back, and she was turned into a pillar of salt" (19:26).

The exact nature of the debauchery that resulted in the destruction of Sodom and Gomorrah is not entirely clear. This is an important observation that should be pointed out to readers of the Bible who insist that they really do know. Read Genesis 19 again. Also consider that, in Luke's Gospel, Jesus warns, "Remember the wife of Lot" (17:32). This may be read today both as a proper interpretation of the Genesis story—after all, it is the interpretation of Jesus himself!—and as a warning to Christians not to turn back to their sin after having claimed new life in Christ through baptism. Pope St. Leo the Great was probably thinking of this warning when, in the fifth century, he admonished, "Christian, remember your dignity."[8]

But why is Lot's wife never named? Was she not a person in her own right? She was clearly a person with free will. Why exactly she was not named is a mystery (old Job's wife got no name either), but clearly it has something to do with how ancient cultures valued (or didn't) women.

But why was she turned to salt? Well, salt appears metaphorically in different places in the Bible to signify, among other things, permanence, loyalty, durability, fidelity, usefulness, value, and purification. All of those are good things. Which does not explain why Lot's wife was turned to salt. It remains a mystery. The Bible can be like that.

What did Jesus have to say about sex?

Not much. Some folks suggest that Jesus spoke clearly and forcibly on all of our age's hot topics. However, a careful reading of Scripture does not support that suggestion.

8. *Sermo* 1 in *Nativitate Domini*, 1–3; PL 54, 190–93: http://www.crossroads initiative.com/library_article/359/Christian_Remember_Your_Dignity__St._ Leo.html.

He never mentioned microprocessors or integrated circuits either.

In Matthew's Gospel, Jesus discusses divorce (see 5:31–32 and 19:9). In Mark (10:11–12) and Luke (16:18), he also addresses the issue. He addresses lust in Matthew (5:27–28).

In his conversation with the Samaritan woman (see John 4:16–18), he speaks of her multiple partners, but it is not entirely clear whether he is rebuking her for a troubled past or revealing himself in such a way as to invite the woman to return to her people with the faith-filled plea: "Come see a man who told me everything I have done. Could he possibly be the Messiah?" (4:29).

In the Bible we read about a woman caught in adultery. The men were about to stone her when Jesus intervened. Had they already stoned the man? Or were only women blamed for adultery back then? And if so, what's up with that?

The interaction of Jesus with the woman caught in adultery (John 8:1–11) is also interesting. One wonders what exactly we learn of ancient cultures when a woman is caught in adultery. How about the guy? She could not have been committing adultery alone. Where was he? Doesn't say.

But Jesus challenges those who wish to stone her: "Let the one among you who is without sin be the first to throw a stone at her." One by one, they go away. Jesus asks her, "Has no one condemned you?" She replies, "No one, sir." Then Jesus says, "Neither do I condemn you. Go, and from now on do not sin any more" (8:7, 10–11). Notice that the story admonishes us not to be judge and jury; it invites healing, forgiveness, and a firm purpose of avoiding future sin.

If we watch Jesus, we learn what he knew as a Jew: do to no one what you yourself despise (Tob 4:15a). Further, Jesus states his desired direction for us, which is both simple to understand and difficult to accomplish: "I give you a new commandment: love one another. As I have loved you, so you also should love one another" (John 13:34). We call this a hard saying of Jesus, not because it is difficult to understand, but, rather, because it is hard to do.

Note that he does not say that we should break into small groups for discussion and say how we really feel about what he has said. Note too that he does not ask us to think it over and act on it if we find it worth our time and while. Nope. He commands. He often invites, but rarely commands. This one, though, is a command, pure and simple.

II

TERMINOLOGY
(AND JUST A LITTLE FASHION)

What is the difference between celibacy and chastity?

Celibacy is the state of remaining unmarried for the sake of the Church or the kingdom of God. Church law requires celibacy for priests of the Latin Rite, brothers, nuns, and sisters. Chastity, on the other hand, is for everyone. To be chaste is to appreciate and employ our sexuality in a manner that is appropriate for our situation in life whether married, single, or celibate.

I saw a bumper sticker that read "Chastity is its own punishment." What's up with that?

That bumper sticker was no doubt written by the same person who insists, "Everything I like is either fattening or sinful." Poor guy either does not like Bach and the Beatles, or finds them sinful and fattening. Hurts to be him. Chastity as its own punishment might be a line some consider funny, but guys should be cautioned against using it when sauntering up to a lovely woman they want to impress. Moving beyond fractured attempts at humor, we should hardly feel

23

punished when seeking to appreciate and employ our sexuality in a manner that is appropriate for our situation in life.

What can I do and still be considered a virgin?

She or he who wants to live by technicalities can assert and insist that those who have not had sexual intercourse are considered virgins, so anything short of that would not compromise their virginity. The prudent person would reframe the question from "How far can I go?" to "Perhaps I am not compromising my virginity, but am I compromising myself and the person I want to become?"

There is a consecrated virgin in my parish. What is that? Isn't it a bit weird?

Not weird at all, just not so common. There are, by some estimates, about two hundred women in the United States, living on their own, working and supporting themselves, who have been consecrated to a life of virginity. The ritual for the consecration explains such a choice as the bishop prays: "[God,] among your many gifts / you give to some the grace of virginity. / Yet the honor of marriage is in no way lessened. / As it was in the beginning, / your first blessing still remains upon this holy union. / Yet your loving wisdom chooses those / who make sacrifice of marriage / for the sake of the love of which it is the sign. / They renounce the joys of human marriage, / but cherish all that it foreshadows." The prayer further explains as it concludes: "They give themselves wholly to Christ, / the Son of the ever-virgin Mary, / and the heavenly Bridegroom of those / who in his honor dedicate themselves to lasting virginity."[9]

---

9. http://www.consecratedvirgins.org/rite.pdf, 7.

When I look at the saints, I notice that the term *virgin* is only used for women. Can't a guy be a virgin?

Both men and women can be virgins. And martyrs, too. It is very interesting that only women saints are referred to as virgins while the unmarried male saints are not. There may be several reasons for this and it may be that none of the reasons are patriarchal or offensive to female sensibilities.

These may be among the reasons that only women saints are referred to as virgins in the Church's life of prayer:

First, pregnancy tips off even the casual observer that the woman in the maternity dress is no longer a virgin. There are no telltale signs for men.

Further, women religious, nuns and sisters, have traditionally employed bridal imagery to speak of the relationship that they have with Christ in their vowed lives. These women religious wear rings to symbolize the image of the virginal bride of Christ. In fact, before the Second Vatican Council, a number of communities of religious women would have new members wear wedding gowns and veils on the day that they professed their vows, changing later into their religious habits. Male religious, priests and brothers, do not employ this wedding imagery to describe or define their own relationship to Christ or the Church (contrary to popular wisdom, priests are not married to the Church). Neither do they wear the symbolic ring; thus, their virginity is not celebrated in the same way as for women.

Can I reclaim virginity or somehow have it restored?

Sorry, virginity cannot be reclaimed. Even Rome cannot give it back to those who mourn the loss. Chastity, however, can be both lost and found.

My roommate was raped. Is she no longer a virgin?

One gives the gift of virginity to another; it cannot be taken. Further, rape is a crime of violence, not an act of passion or intimacy. Any fair-minded person should certainly insist that one who suffers rape is a victim who has given neither assent nor virginity to the attacker.

What is the difference between fornication and adultery?

The unmarried person who has sexual intercourse commits fornication. The married person who has sexual intercourse with a person other than her or his spouse commits adultery. So one bed could hold both an adulterer and a fornicator at the same sinful moment.

What about incest? What makes it wrong?

Incest is sexual activity between family members. It is a taboo in most cultures and is illegal in many jurisdictions and in every developed country. The degree of kinship varies from place to place in considerations of incest. Most jurisdictions prohibit brothers, sisters, mothers, fathers, aunts, and uncles from marrying; in some places in the United States, the prohibition against marrying extends to first cousins.

When incest involves someone under age, it is sexual abuse. Many commentators suggest that incest tends to lead to trauma and psychological damage. Additionally, birth defects are more common to children born of incest.

Incest is not consistent with a biblical or a Catholic view of the purposes of sexuality. It would be difficult to see any relationship between acts of incest and the celebration of human dignity.

What about transvestites? What are they all about? Are they the same as transsexuals? How will it harm me if I meet one? Do I need to be afraid that I might become one?

A transvestite is a man or woman who finds sexual pleasure by dressing in the clothing of the opposite sex. Such behavior is often seen as deviant. Others regard it as quirky. Some married couples experiment with cross-dressing as they seek mutual pleasure. It should be noted that a transvestite is not necessarily homosexual.

Men who dress as women are sometimes said to be "in drag." There seems to be no corresponding term for women who dress as men. I am not aware of any argument that suggests that the practice is a condition that can be caught, so you need not fear becoming a transvestite against your will. The practice, as for so much of human behavior, could be sinful but need not necessarily be. It is a matter that might be discussed with one's confessor or spiritual director.

A transsexual believes that she or he was born into the wrong gender. Some men, for example, live as women and vice-versa. Others seek operations to remedy their difficulty. Theirs is a complex situation or problem, and those who suffer from it deserve our compassion as they seek, with all available help, to understand how to live in a way that is in keeping with our shared human dignity.

Is a fetish always a sin?

A fetish is a fixation on an object or body part. It could be a way to add spice to a relationship, or it may become an obsession with serious consequences. If a fetish interferes with one's life and relationships, this should be a signal that

finding some help might be in order, either in the reconciliation chapel or with a counselor, or both.

Is there still such a thing as an orgy? My friend claims that there is and that orgies harm no one as long as they are held in private. Could this be true?

An orgy is a group event in which participants
promiscuously participate in sexual activity. It often features drunkenness, dancing, and song. Not much about
this sounds private. There was much talk of orgies in the
1970s; how often they may have occurred and where is
not known. At least not by me. Your friend is, one might
suppose, entitled to her opinion that orgies harm no one,
but fairness would suggest that the burden of proof would
lie with her. It is difficult to imagine how any good at all
could come of such a scenario, or how anyone might imagine a way that an orgy could be in keeping with human
dignity.

Why are women's pants designed so low that you can always see their belly buttons? Whatever happened to waists?

Your mothers and grandmothers were asked the same
question by their parents when empire-waist dresses were in
fashion. There is no accounting for taste, and apparently there
never has been, as the Latin adage shows: *De gustibus non est
disputandum* ("there is no dispute concerning tastes").

Why do some boys and men think that wearing their pants half down around their butts is attractive?

Who does not appreciate seeing a young man in a hurry, clutching his waistband in one hand and seeking balance with his other arm? The variety of boxer shorts with wild colors and crazy prints one can spy on an average day might raise our hearts and minds to consider higher art.

I did raise a question of taste one recent day with a young man who came to pay a call in my office. When I viewed his, well, preposterous get-up, I asked (kindly and without judgment!) the attraction for him of a particular piece of apparel. He was sad for my obtuseness, so explained patiently, "Father, this is the style for young men." The only true issue of morality with regard to fashion is raised in the next question.

My grandmother uses the terms *modest* and *immodest*. Is this because she was born in a different century?

Perhaps. And she may have been reading Pope St. Leo the Great as well. Leo, an early Church father and a doctor of the Church who reigned in the middle of the fifth century, wrote: "Christian, remember your dignity, and now that you share in God's own nature, do not return by sin to your former base condition. Bear in mind who is your head and of whose body you are a member. Do not forget that you have been rescued from the power of darkness and brought into the light of God's kingdom.

"Through the sacrament of baptism you have become a temple of the Holy Spirit. Do not drive away so great a guest by evil conduct and become again a slave to the devil, for your liberty was bought by the blood of Christ."[10]

---

10. *Sermo* 1 in *Nativitate Domini*, 1–3; PL 54, 190–93: http://www.crossroads initiative.com/library_article/359/Christian_Remember_Your_Dignity__St._ Leo.html.

What Gram really wants is for you to remember your own dignity, and not to squander it as you pursue fashion or friends. This means dressing and behaving in ways that will not make you cringe when, years from now, family photos are passed around, Facebook accounts are resurrected, and stories are told.

III

HOMOSEXUALITY

I've seen some Web sites and T-shirts that are big on listing abominations, even suggesting that God might harbor hate for certain groups of people and even crustaceans. Can it be possible, as they seem to suggest, that God hates either homosexuals or shellfish?

Not possible. God is all about love. Let us not forget what we have read in Genesis: God surveyed all of creation, "and he found it very good" (1:31). This includes people as well as crustaceans.

The Old Testament Book of Leviticus warns, "But of the various creatures that crawl or swim in the water, whether in the sea or in the rivers, all those that lack either fins or scales are loathsome for you, and you shall treat them as loathsome" (11:10–11). Some translations are even more graphic, using the word *abomination* to describe what seems to be someone having a shrimp dinner.

Leviticus and Deuteronomy instructed the Israelite people about separating themselves from what they had learned or practiced while slaves in Egypt. Both of these biblical books are about contrast and separation, distinctions and differences. Scholars and holy people help us to interpret and to understand, and we must be very cautious not to adopt a simplistic approach that will lead us, not just into error, but into lapses of justice and charity as well.

Leviticus 17—26 gives what is commonly called the "Holiness Code," a collection of many laws on a number of different topics, including a large section on sexual activities. Some Christians cite certain of these laws in a tendentious manner, without pausing to reflect on the curious fact that they themselves are willing to obey some laws (or eager to insist that others obey them), while ignoring other problematic commands.

If we wish to understand the many issues about and relating to homosexuality, we cannot insist that Leviticus 20:13 is all we need to know or quote.

Reading the Bible is a complex task. Pius XII issued his encyclical *Divino afflante Spiritu* in 1943 and invited the serious study of Scripture, insisting that if we wish to understand God's Word, we must seek to understand the ancient cultures to which the Word was first announced and the languages in which the Word was recorded. Faithful Catholics, and all people of good will, are thus given notice that a casual application of proof texts may well not be a faithful way to read God's enduring, transforming Word or to put that Word into practice.

Do let's remember that one Leviticus verse inspired the inscription on the Liberty Bell: "Proclaim LIBERTY throughout all the Land unto all the Inhabitants thereof Lev. XXV X."[11]

All this being said, it might be a helpful exercise to imagine God's delight in watching a homosexual person

---

11. The NAB translation is: "This fiftieth year you shall make sacred by proclaiming liberty in the land for all its inhabitants. It shall be a jubilee for you, when every one of you shall return to his own property, every one to his own family estate" (Lev 25:10).

enjoy a shrimp cocktail on the Sabbath: imitating God on that very first Sabbath by resting from labors and enjoying the wonders of creation.

So, then, I guess it isn't true that all homosexuals go to hell?

Good guess. But, like any other human person, a homosexual person can insist that she or he would like to go to hell. But, really, who wants to go there? While we certainly can choose to go to hell, we will not be sent there because we were born with blond hair, brown eyes, or an attraction to persons of our same gender. So, with regard to hell: exercise your right to choose!

Is it true that homosexuals are made, not born?

No. You may be confusing this erroneous idea with a famous statement from Tertullian (c. 160–c. 220), an early Church father: "Christians are made, not born."[12] It seems to be the firmly held hypothesis of the scientific community that some individuals are born homosexual; thus, it is nature rather than nurture that decides how we develop. Those who argue against this hypothesis rarely have evidence. Those who insist that the Bible is their evidence are incorrect.

Why does the Church consider homosexuality wrong?

The Church does not consider it wrong to be a homosexual person. The Church is careful to distinguish between homosexual persons and acts. In the Catholic tradition, sex-

---

12. *Apologeticus*, xviii: http://www.ccel.org/ccel/schaff/anf03.toc.html.

ual intercourse is reserved for marriage. Genital expressions of sexuality outside of marriage are not considered in keeping with the purposes of human sexuality as those purposes have been elucidated in Genesis and the constant teaching of the Church.

What is the difference between homosexual orientation and homosexual acts?

Those persons with a same-sex attraction are considered homosexual. Homosexual acts are the genital expression of that attraction.

Why can marriage not be between two people of the same gender?

The purposes of marriage include not just the love between husband and wife, but also the business of procreation, the design by which future generations of tithe-payers and taxpayers are born. There are and have always been other relationships and family structures in which God is honored and humankind is sanctified, but the Church understands marriage to be divinely instituted; consequently, it has no power to change the definition.

While the Church insists that homosexual people be treated with the same dignity and respect as all God's people, same-sex unions are not seen as possessing all of the qualities necessary to constitute a marriage. Undoubtedly, however, a true theological understanding of how homosexuality is or is not part of God's plan is incomplete, and the discussion will continue.

Is it fair that homosexuals are expected to be celibate while heterosexuals can choose?

This is an important and difficult question. Heterosexual people can choose to be single, married, or celibate. Traditionally, homosexual people have only been able to choose to be single or celibate. So, if somewhere between 2 and 10 percent of all people are homosexual, as is often claimed, must all of them live without expressing that sexuality? This has been the constant teaching of the Church.

Today, many people and certain other Christian denominations are struggling to find other answers to this question. As is often the case when discussions are new and ideas are still being formed, some answers may be wrong or suspect. Some answers or proposed solutions seem not to respect Church teaching in the fervent wish that any partnership be regarded as a marriage.

The Catholic Church regards marriage as a unique institution in which the love of a man and a woman goes beyond itself and, in cooperation with God, may issue forth in new life. This is not to say that other relationships are not life-giving or life-affirming; we all know that God works not just through marriage but through all of us and our many, varied relationships to create the future of the world.

It is both fair and safe to say that the causes of homosexuality have not yet been fully considered. The exigencies of our own age suggest that this is an issue that, while it seems to push the limits of moral theology, requires us, as St. Benedict puts it in the prologue of his *Rule for Monasteries*, to listen with the ear of our hearts. Our shared aim as Christians must be to seek answers and explanations that celebrate what it means to be fully alive, beloved children of the Most High God, and brothers and sisters together in the unity that is the Body of Christ.

Whose fault is it if I am gay? If I tell my parents, will they have reason to disown me?

How we are born is not a fault: it is just who and how we are. Some incorrectly presume that homosexuals chose their orientation or are perhaps recruited. Others worry about social stigma or fear the pain or prejudice that their children may suffer. The United States Conference of Catholic Bishops addresses parents in a remarkable letter, "Always Our Children: A Pastoral Message to Parents of Homosexual Children and Suggestions for Pastoral Ministers."[13] This letter is a very helpful resource, and even the title speaks to the concern of those who ask about disowning or being disowned.

Pope John Paul II also extended a healing hand that should be very encouraging to those who suffer. He wrote, "An even more generous, intelligent and prudent pastoral commitment, modeled on the Good Shepherd, is called for in cases of families which, often independently of their own wishes and through pressures of various other kinds, find themselves faced by situations which are objectively difficult."[14]

Miss Manners advises that, when introduced to a homosexual couple, one should say, "How do you do? How do you do?"[15] I have two questions: Do people really speak like that these days? And, should I not speak out and voice my and the Church's opposition to sodomy?

Listen to Miss Manners. She is not simply flip, but invites us to focus on the real issues at hand and not periph-

---

13. http://www.usccb.org/laity/always.shtml.

14. John Paul II, *On the Family*, 1981, no. 77.

15. Judith Martin, *Miss Manners' Guide to Excruciatingly Correct Behavior* (New York: Atheneum, 1982), 67.

eral concerns. If you feel obliged to shout out your abhorrence for what you feel is bad or immoral behavior when you meet people socially, perhaps you are a prophet. But remember that prophets are not self-anointed; they are appointed by God. Unless you are a card-carrying member of a Guild of Prophets, it would be more prudent and more socially acceptable simply to greet those you meet rather than announce what you presume to be their sinfulness.

Given the prevalence of sinfulness among people, you would be very busy in your shout-outs. But if you are concerned only with some groups and not with all God's people, you would not be an equal-opportunity prophet. We might find inspiration in the psalms: "The LORD is just and loves just deeds; / the upright shall see his face" (11:7).

My lesbian daughter often concludes our conversations by telling me to "take a chill pill." I routinely say that the term *chill pill* suggests that she is perpetually mired in the 1980s. What do you think she is really saying?

Your daughter may well have in mind the picture of Jesus inviting the apostles: "Come away by yourselves to a deserted place and rest a while" (Mark 6:31). He had just learned about the death of his precursor, John the Baptist, and was undoubtedly sad and distressed. Those who are involved in the difficult dialogue about understanding human sexuality and how we deal with difference and differences must often feel a sadness and distress much like that of Jesus. We should follow his lead and be sure that we have time for quiet reflection, prayer, and rest in between our bouts of spirited, charitable dialogue.

Our very human tendency is to think that the solutions or answers we see as good and just today should be the model for the rest of the Church and all the world. Your daughter seems to recognize that in your discussions, you are exploring the frontiers of moral theology and ethics and of what it means to be fully human. How homosexuality is or is not part of God's plan has been discussed out loud only very recently in the course of human history.

In 1896, Lord Alfred Douglas coined the phrase "the love that dare not speak its name" in his poem "Two Loves." Douglas and Oscar Wilde, a nineteenth-century author, were cautious in describing their relationship because homosexuality was then a criminal offense in England. Wilde, in fact, was convicted of "gross indecency" with other men and imprisoned for two years.

In June 1969, the Stonewall riots, a series of demonstrations against a police raid at the Stonewall Inn in New York City's Greenwich Village, may be the first instance in American history when homosexual people united to speak out against a system that they felt persecuted them. Many regard this moment as the beginning of the gay rights movement.

If homosexuality has only been openly discussed for not much more than forty of Christianity's two-thousand-year tradition (and who knows why exactly we were so late in beginning the discussion), we can hardly expect to arrive at the fullness of truth before tomorrow's first coffee break. Commentators on the Church often point out that the United States is a microwave culture; we expect results in seconds or minutes. Rome, on the other hand, is more like a Crock-Pot, thinking and moving in blocks of centuries rather than days. The Latin adage *festina lente*, "make haste slowly," reminds us—as the discussions continue, as we seek to understand the truth—that we should be about our learning and our teaching in the proper way, and not hurriedly or heedlessly. Even though the matter is urgent, we must be thorough in our consideration and deliberations.

In prescribing the "chill pill," your daughter seems to reveal herself as a thoughtful person intent on carrying on discussions in a relaxed and life-affirming manner. She clearly knows that how we live, and how we make our feelings and opinions known, reveal what kind of people we are. When Jesus tells us, "By their fruits you will know them" (Matt 7:16), he was speaking of both false prophets and good trees.

You and your daughter seem to understand that the witness of holy lives will move both earth and Church more forcibly than any well-crafted argument or mean-spirited remark.

She could, however, update her antique pharmacological reference.

IV

SEX IN THE CITY

What's so wrong about masturbation?

Genesis gives us the idea of what human sexuality is about and what it is for when it tells the story of creation. These purposes include expressing and celebrating the love between husband and wife, as well as procreating, the business by which earth and Church are continually populated. Solo sexual pleasure is not mentioned in Genesis or elsewhere in the Scriptures or Tradition, and has thus seemed to be outside the number of ways that Christians might seek to participate in the mystery of God.

In the Song of Songs, or the Song of Solomon, we read of the lover, King Solomon, who comes to meet his bride. As she waits, she laments: "On my bed at night I sought him / whom my heart loves— / I sought him but I did not find him." What to do while waiting? Her solution: "I will rise then and go about the city; / in the streets and crossings I will seek / Him whom my heart loves" (Song 3:1–2).

The lesson from the Song of Songs seems to be that there are any number of ways to meet our needs, some more in keeping with holiness and wholeness than others. Sometimes you just need to go take a walk or a cold shower.

41

If I am careful to avoid sexually transmitted diseases, as well as sexually transmitted infections, what's so wrong about a random procession of sexual partners?

One does get the idea from prime-time television that a date that does not end in bed is the waste of a good evening. This is not our Christian view. If we are all about pleasure but not about goodness, we are surely doomed. Further, while we can celebrate the fact that God forgives, we often mourn the reality that nature punishes.

My girlfriend and I have limited incomes and we find sex an inexpensive form of entertainment. What's it to you?

Heavens. Have you two not heard that the Art Institute of Chicago has free general admission every Thursday night from 5 till 8 p.m.? But thanks for asking, "What's it to you?" Our expressions of sexuality and the way we fulfill our desires often have an impact, not just on ourselves, but also on our families, the Church, and the rest of society. It rarely is only all about you. So, as a member of both Church and society, you might want to ask, for example, how an unintended pregnancy might have an impact on others: the child, the grandparents, social-service providers, and tax-payers. Or the impact of an STD or STI on all concerned. Or the trauma that may be associated with one partner having expectations not shared by the other. Or the guilt one or the other may feel in recognizing that what the Church views as participating in the mystery of God and creation is, in your view, just a cheaper alternative to Saturday night or Tuesday afternoon at the movies.

While you think your entertainment is free, others would assert that it is certainly not without cost.

I have a rich life of fantasy. Should I feel guilty?

Our imagination can be a rich source of goodness and a place where we meet God, or a site where evil finds a home. Goodness does not call us to guilt. When we do feel guilty, we should heed the call to examine our days and our deeds. And our fantasies, too. Perhaps a visit to the reconciliation chapel or confessional is in order.

What about professional athletes and stars of stage and screen who have serial and sometimes unwilling sex partners and then apologize all over the place? Who do they think they are, and what's up with that?

Being rich or famous or good at a sport does not create a different set of standards by which one can live. And whether or not they consider themselves role models, the rich and famous are bound by our common humanity, as are we all, to be good examples to all those who may observe us.

How far does it have to go to be sex abuse?

Someone who is underage cannot give true or legal consent to sexual activity with someone older. Depending on the jurisdiction, underage usually means under eighteen to get married, join the military, or give consent to sexual activity; or under twenty-one to buy or consume alcohol. Similarly, when a person is approached by someone who has power over him or her because of rank or position, that person also may not be in a position to give true consent. Either of these situations could lead to sexual abuse.

Any person made uncomfortable by an advance from another should say firmly that she or he is uncomfortable and make every effort to retreat to a safe place. This situation too could lead to abuse. Do not be afraid to call for help if you feel threatened. Do not be timid about reporting threats or abuse to the appropriate authorities.

Anyone who is touched in an inappropriate or sexual way without her or his express consent may be or become a victim of sexual abuse. Victims or possible victims should know that they are not at fault. Those who feel in danger of being victimized should notify the appropriate authorities without delay.

Those who would harm the young or the vulnerable are a grave scourge for all of society. There must be no tolerance for inappropriate, criminal, or sinful sexual activity or threats that harm or might harm the vulnerable among us.

The priest in my parish is not a nice man; at least I do not think so. We'd really be better off without him. I am thinking of calling our bishop's hotline to say that this priest propositioned me in the confessional and abused me sexually when I was a teenager, even though he did neither. My small lie might get us a better pastor. Do you see a flaw in my plan?

Your proposal should shiver the timbers of any person of good will. There is never an excuse to defame an innocent person or to blight his good name. Further, a priest who is unjustly accused may never recover his position, his reputation, or his equilibrium. The ramifications of the evil deed you propose are horrifying. Please be honorable.

I am unmarried. If I have sex but do not use birth control, can I consider myself a good Catholic? Or half good?

Would you settle for half-baked? When Pope Paul VI penned the encyclical *Humanae Vitae* and famously spoke out against artificial means of birth control, he was not writing to young people in the back seat of a 1968 Ford Falcon with fogged-up windows, parked in a dark, quiet spot. His proposal was about seeking perfection in Christian marriage; he did not provide a checklist for those who see premarital sex as one more thrilling experience.

Your question suggests that it might be time for you to reconsider both *Humanae Vitae* and your own approach to sexuality in the context of the rapidly unfolding new century. But first, review the purposes of sexual activity in light of what it means to be a whole person seeking holiness.

My boyfriend and I are engaged to be married. What about sex? Do we have to wait?

As a relationship is not a marriage before the public vows are made, the Church teaches that a "marriage that is *ratum et consummatum* can be dissolved by no human power and by no cause, except by death" (Code of Canon Law, 1141). A marriage that is *ratum* is one in which bride and groom have pronounced their vows in the presence of the Church's minister and witnesses. A marriage is usually *consummatum* after the wedding night. But a marriage cannot be consummated before the public vows are made; so, until then, the activity you describe is premarital sex.

You might argue that the premarital sex of an engaged couple is better than sleeping around with a procession of strangers. Expect to be asked, "But is it virtuous?"

How about living together?

As a marriage cannot be consummated before the public vows are made, you are describing a reality other than marriage. Many of the ways in which that reality is described sound judgmental: shacked up, living in sin, and so on. Perhaps you have a more felicitous description?

But living apart is more expensive.

Perhaps. Depends on how you count costs.

My spouse insists on referring to our oldest child as living in sin or being shacked up. He says that he is only calling it as he sees it. I do not find his approach helpful. Do you?

If your spouse is seeking to cut off any dialogue before it begins, or perhaps intends to provoke the adult child into digging in her or his heels just to make the point that the parent is not in charge, then congratulations are in order for a job well done. If there is some other intent, the results must be disappointing.

If one's partner in conversation were to object to one term or another for any reason at all, why would we not use an alternative term? A new term will not create a new reality, just as a rose by any other name would still smell as sweet. I am just guessing here, but I'll bet that you, the questioner, are a mom and the other is the dad. Sometimes we guys can be contrary and difficult, as perhaps you may have noticed. Dad here is ornery and provocative, winning no points with his offspring and apparently making no inroads toward changed behavior of, or even conversation with, said offspring.

He is also failing to reflect the kind of tender compassion and eagerness to listen that we see in Jesus when in conversation with the Samaritan woman.

The Catholic Church makes little girls dress up like brides when they are seven for first communion, don't they? And in certain cultures, when they are fifteen, for *quinciñera*. Is that good? And what's the *quinciñera* really about? It looks like an announcement that a girl is ready to rock. Isn't fifteen a little young to be put on the market?

Yes, in some places first communicants may dress in white and may wear veils. This is not a universal rule but a local or family custom. It should be viewed not as sexualizing children in a religious ritual, but rather as suggesting both purity and festivity when preparing to meet Christ in the sacraments. The white gown suggests not bridal business, but recalls our baptism and the purity it imparts.

It should be noted, too, that some folks are tempted or even sidetracked by trendy, materialistic concerns. They mistakenly seek another consumer-oriented occasion in anticipation of a future wedding, seeing first communion as a dress rehearsal complete with mini-bride and white dress. This obscures what is to be the focus of both first communion and marriage. St. Paul reminds us of the real message for both occasions: Keep your eyes on the prize (see Phil 3:14).

The *quinciñera* is a ceremony in some Latin cultures that celebrates a girl's fifteenth birthday and entry into young adulthood. The point is not to put her on the market; that sounds something like a cattle auction or child abuse. St. Paul will help refine that thought: "Think of what is above" (Col 3:2). You'll notice a candle at the *quinciñera*;

it is a reminder of both the girl's baptismal candle and the paschal candle, because at the ceremony she will renew the baptismal promises that her parents and godparents made in her name when she was carried in their arms to the church for baptism.

Both events should highlight, not obscure, the link to our baptism.

How do I know if my behavior is moral or immoral? And why should I care?

Remember that in our consciences, we discover a law that we have not invented but must obey. This voice calls us to love, to do what is good, and to avoid evil. This call is a law inscribed in the heart by God, and our dignity lies in observing it; this is why we should and do care.

In heeding the call of conscience, Christians are joined to all other people of good will in the search for truth and for correct solutions to moral problems that are both personal and social in nature. So we do not depend on what might feel or seem good to us, but we recognize the need to educate ourselves and inform our consciences as we seek to become better persons. This is the work of a lifetime. The Scriptures and the Church assist us.

Is it enough for me just to say that I'll follow my conscience?

We must always seek to follow our consciences. And we are also bound to see that our consciences are well informed and up-to-date. This is a broad order and the work of a lifetime. The task of the Church and the purpose of Church teachings are to assist us in our duty.

We judge our intentions and our acts, as well as the circumstances, as moral or immoral based on the effects the act has on ourselves and others, hoping always that these effects are about goodness rather than evil. We should care about all of this if we care about quality of life, the presence of grace, and our participation in the task of renewing the earth as we prepare to meet the Lord when he comes in glory.

If I should happen to sin sexually (it can happen, I know), or if I feel that I somehow have just not been my best self, how can I go to confession to a priest who is celibate? Won't he be embarrassed or confused? Would it be better simply to presume that God forgives me? And anyway, it has been so long since I have gone to confession, I hate to just jump in and start talking about sex and have him think I'm a pervert or something. And I think I forgot how to start.

Unless the priest hearing your confession was ordained only this morning and grew up in a Baggie, you'll not tell him anything that will make him blush.

Many Catholic people have anxiety about approaching the sacrament of reconciliation. Some fear that the priest will judge them. But that is not why he is there. The point is pardon and peace. The priest judges the act, not the person.

The formula is simple. Entering the appointed spot, usually a confessional or reconciliation chapel (though the sacrament can be celebrated anywhere), the penitent makes the Sign of the Cross, and says, "Bless me, Father, for I have sinned." Usually, she or he will say how long it has been since last confessing, and then mention the sins committed and how often each has occurred. The penitent concludes, saying, "I am sorry for these and all the sins of my past life." She or he might also say the Act of Contrition (see page 88) at this point.

The priest may comment, offer encouragement, give a penance, and invite the penitent to express sorrow and contrition. Finally, the priest, with hands extended over the penitent, says the prayer of absolution.

The focus of the sacrament is not guilt, but grace. And grace, as those who have gone before remind, will lead us on.

Are some things always wrong, or does it just depend on what I think or feel? As long as there are no victims, I mean.

Yes, some things are just wrong, always and everywhere and for everyone. Feeling that rape can be a virtue would not make it so. You might have thought that there were no victims. This would not mean that there truly were no victims.

Now that we have agreed that there are, in fact, objectively immoral acts, we should continue the discussion of what those acts might include. We should seek to do good acts, avoid evil or destructive acts, and avoid also what back in the day was called "near occasions of sin." There are places we should not be and opportunities we should not seek out.

V

SEX ON CAMPUS

My roommate is on the football team and has never had sex. Is that gay or what?

Or what. Students and unmarried young adults who are not engaged in an endless round of sexual activity are really not all that exceptional. They are part of the growing cohort that seeks to understand what it means to be human before seeking human pleasure. Honesty and respect for virtue are at issue here. In a recent class, one young man volunteered, "I do not intend to have sex until my wedding night." Usually in classroom discussion of such matters, we seek out the principles that are foundational for us, rather than confessing how our own activities do or do not reflect what we have read in the Gospel. But this young man's revelation was met with respect and even admiration. A football player and an excellent student, he is also sturdily built, affable, and movie-star handsome, so perhaps these attributes caused people to attend respectfully to what he said. Or maybe it was the fact that he was bigger than most. But he certainly suggested that real virtue can be found in real men and seemed proud to be one of those men. Good for him.

And please stop referring to things you do not understand as "gay." There is no gaiety following such an utterance.

51

What's so wrong about being friends with benefits?

Casual sex will produce no benefits, will complicate or ruin friendships, and the consequences may well be devastating. Because you may feel that everyone is doing it is no assurance that they are, that it is either right, life giving, or life affirming, or that you will find in it the true path to happiness.

I feel uncomfortable around people who are different from me. And I mean not just the prudes, but also those who flaunt their sexuality. What should I do?

When in doubt, both refer to and treat them as persons. It's neither difficult nor dangerous. "Hi, Melanie. Ready for our algebra quiz?" "Hey, Dylan, your faux-hawk is looking especially upright today." Look at their faces as you speak, and pay attention when they answer.

My girlfriend goes to a public school and the prom is coming up. I want to take her, but there are two trannie boys who will be there as a couple. Can we go to the prom if they are there, or should we stay home and play Monopoly?

By "trannie boys," I presume you mean either transvestites or transsexuals. A transsexual believes that she or he was born into the wrong gender. Some men, for example, live as women and vice-versa. Others seek operations to remedy their difficulty. Theirs is a complex situation or problem, and those who suffer from it deserve our compassion as they seek, with all available help, to understand how to live in a way that is in keeping with our shared human dignity. Transvestites are those who dress as members of the opposite sex, and do so for a whole complex of reasons.

You, your girlfriend, and your parents should discuss what compassion and enlightened self-interest might look like in your situation. To attend the prom need not compromise your virtue in any way. Staying home alone to play Monopoly, on the other hand, may well put you at risk; you could find yourselves in a situation that could be a near occasion of sin. And that might not be good.

What about sex education in our schools? Should I be for or against it?

It depends. There is much in a sex-education curriculum that could be both enlightening and helpful. Some approaches might be harmful. For example, some educators seem to confuse their personal opinions with the truth. Should this be the case, not only is the sex-education curriculum at risk, but so also are the laws of physics.

In my sex-ed class in high school, our teacher says sexual love is a power source. Does the Church agree, or is my mom correct again when she says I am being taught dangerous stuff in that course?

Yes, the Church certainly sees sexual love as a power source; it drives the marriage engine. This thought should not frighten you, and should console your mom. If it is not clear that this is what your teacher means, by all means, speak up and ask! It should be apparent that some power tools are not appropriate for use by high school students; certain pieces of machinery and sex are numbered among them.

I am a college student and think that, as long as no one gets hurt and there are no victims, all else is fine and fair. Agree?

Disagree. How do you propose to guarantee that no one will be hurt and that no one will be victimized? Giving one's consent to an activity does not guarantee that one will be free from harm.

My theology professor cautions that we should not make someone else's blueprint the model for our lives. As I am not an architecture student, I am not sure what he means. Are you?

Your theology professor is suggesting, I think, that if someone says, "Well, we'll all grow up to date, get married, and have 2.5 kids, a house in the suburbs, a career as an actuary, and a gold watch in retirement," you need not buy into being part of the "we'll all." Your dreams and your journey may take shape differently and perfectly in keeping with what it means to be a full human person seeking to conform her or his life to God's will. As we seek to do the divine will, we soon find that one size does not fit all.

My boyfriend won't sleep with me. He says it is because he respects me. Does that mean that when I'm married, my husband won't respect me? I'm so confused.

Your boyfriend understands that respect for you as a child of God entails avoiding some activities as not appropriate to his current situation in life. His approach is in keeping with Church teaching about the informed use of our sexual powers.

Because your future husband, let us fervently hope, will love you and respect you, you and he will express your love sexually in a way that will build up both of you and perhaps issue forth in new life, children.

It is natural to feel confused. We should be slow to act in confusion as that is often when we make mistakes. Perhaps you'll find it helpful to take your confusion to prayer. Maybe chapter X will help!

Is it ever a good idea to have sex without love?

No. Not ever. Now break into small groups and discuss.

My boyfriend bought me a T-shirt that his fraternity was selling; the caption on it reads, "I ♥ Consensual Sex." He asked me why I have not worn it, and I said I could wear it next Sunday when we go to church and have brunch with his parents. Now he is mad. Would you wear it? To church?

Your boyfriend is a relativist. If it were good to wear that shirt, it would be good to wear it in front of God and mom. What is he hiding? He might insist that the shirt really means, "I do not heart rape." If it really meant only that, why would he want you to wear it to a frat party but not to brunch? Both he and the shirt should say what they mean.

Do guys ever lie about what they consider their sexual conquests? In the locker room, maybe?

Does Michelangelo's *David* have a marble butt? David's chiseled features are attributes to be admired; the lies, not so much. But, perhaps influenced by television and popular culture, guys often will exaggerate their claims of conquests and maybe even confuse their fantasies with their actual sexual history. Our commonly held hope is that they will grow up, as did St. Paul: "When I was a child, I used to talk as a child, think as a child, reason as a child; when I became a man, I put aside childish things" (1 Cor 13:12).

My mother told me that the best birth control is to hold an aspirin tablet between my knees. Could she be serious? Aspirin?

Your mother has an understanding of human nature and the proclivities of the human heart that would have brought a smile to the solemn lips of Pope Paul VI. While he condemned artificial means of birth control, he would have agreed with mom that her solution is both natural and inspired.

VI

PORNOGRAPHY, PROSTITUTION, AND INTERNET ISSUES

Ever since I have started watching reruns of *Friends* on cable, I want to start watching porn like Joey and Chandler used to do. My girlfriend says, "Gross!" What's wrong with a little porn?

Did Joey and Chandler not sometimes have the good sense to be embarrassed about their pastime (or was it an addiction?), which treats sex as a commodity? Your girlfriend says "gross" and you seem not to address the charge. Can you really suggest that it is not gross? Can you find any virtue in it? The titillation you experience is, well, cheap. Do you want to be that kind of guy?

Isn't pornography, like prostitution, just a victimless crime?

Who says there are no victims in pornography or prostitution? Is there an enlightened soul left alive who would not consider prostitutes among the most victimized of God's people? Both the boyfriend and girlfriend in the question above seem to be victims. Not to mention that pathetic pair,

57

Joey and Chandler. And what of those who, pardon the expression, star in the films? Their exposure to STDs and STIs would seem to be one issue. The coarsening of human sensibilities another. The diminishment of the sanctity of sexual activity yet another. And when children are involved? Mercy! It seems that everyone involved can be considered victims. There are no heroes or saints in either industry, just boatloads of victims. Thoughtful people will not add to the victims' burdens by consuming their wares.

I read that sex is a commodity nowadays. If I can buy other commodities, why is it wrong to buy sex?

Commodities are products of the earth or articles of commerce. They include wheat, cattle, and gold. Speculators buy and sell commodities. For example, if you thought inclement weather might destroy the corn crop, you could ask your broker to purchase as much as you can afford. If you are correct in your speculation and the price of corn rises dramatically, your investment is worth much more. So one can buy pork belly futures and be perfectly moral.

Commodities are about exchange, wealth for goods or products or services. In that sense, one might mistakenly suggest that sex is a commodity. But human dignity is not for sale; no person of good will should confuse a prostitute for a commodities trader.

As long as my porn is not illegal, how can it be immoral?

Only a student on the first day of an ethics class might suggest that legality is a guarantee of morality. Much of what is lawful can provide rich opportunity for sin.

I have heard it claimed that pornography debases me and the people who produce it. How can that be?

Anything that contributes to making us less than we might be coarsens us. To be coarse is not a virtue. Participation in or paying for the debasement of another compounds one's guilt.

Is it always a sin to use Internet sites or dating services to meet people to date? And even if it isn't exactly sinful, is it a good plan?

People might meet in church or in the produce aisle or in school. Back in the day, some met through personal ads in various newspapers. Today, many meet through Internet services and sites. Great numbers of these sites set out to provide real services to good people. Sites that might be dubious or intended to lead one astray are usually easily identified. Raunchy sites cannot conceal what they are. If one avoids the sites that do not celebrate human dignity, morality is probably not at issue, though prudence is. Be careful where and when you agree to meet a stranger.

Can I trust that Internet sites, prime-time television programs, and late-night comedians speak with authority on matters of the heart and of sexuality?

Virtue is usually not as funny as sin. Go figure. But while going for and getting the laugh is an art form to be appreciated, the laugh line does not always correspond with an informed view of human sexuality as a path in the search for holiness. One is probably well advised to take little advice on matters of sex or heart from entertainers.

Are all opinions equally valid, and is the Church just one more blog to consider?

In a world where every opinion is king or queen, the Church is just a little voice. But consider the prophet Elijah's experience. The Lord told Elijah to stand on the mountain as he, the Lord, would be passing by. "A strong and heavy wind was rending the mountains and crushing rocks before the LORD—but the LORD was not in the wind. After the wind there was an earthquake—but the LORD was not in the earthquake. After the earthquake there was fire—but the LORD was not in the fire. After the fire there was a tiny whispering sound. When he heard this, Elijah hid his face in his cloak and went and stood at the entrance of the cave (1 Kgs 19:11–13)."

Wisdom may well be found when and where we least expect. We should keep our eyes on cataclysms and our ears attuned to whispering sounds. The tiny sounds we should process in the sanctuary of our consciences.

VII

SEX AND RELATIONSHIPS

My girlfriend and I really like each other, but we are really more in like than in love. We don't think we want to be together forever and so we don't talk of marriage. But now she is pregnant. Since we don't want marriage and also don't want someone else to raise our child, we feel abortion is a good plan for us. Is it still a sin?

Yes, it seriously sounds like a serious sin. And you may well be guilty of any number of other sins. In fact, you may have scaled the summit of selfish narcissism. But you may also be discovering that it really isn't always all about you. Now it is also about a developing child, not just your son or daughter, but a true child of God, who also has his or her own human rights. Our behavior always has consequences, and with your particular consequence comes a call to exercise true responsibility. Grow up; attempt to discern what will best serve all concerned; do the right thing; seek the abundant help that is available to bring your unborn child to birth.[16] The

---

16. The following Web sites belong to well-established organizations that exist to help with unplanned pregnancies:
Birthright International / www.birthright.org / 800-550-4900
National Right to Life / www.nrlc.org/abortion/help.html
The Nurturing Network / www.nurturingnetwork.org / 800-TNN-4MOM
Abortion Alternatives / www.abortionalternatives.com

confessional was invented for folks such as you; view it as a gift, not as a threat or punishment. (See chapter IV!) You and your girlfriend can together make a firm purpose of amendment.

I asked a woman from my office out for coffee. She wore a T-shirt that read, "I am a virgin. But this is an old T-shirt." Is it possible for a man and a woman to be friends and not have a sexual relationship?

It is indeed possible. What your coffee partner has in mind may be something else entirely. Perhaps the author of the First Epistle of Peter was thinking of a similar person when he wrote, "Be sober and vigilant. Your opponent the devil is prowling around like a roaring lion looking for (someone) to devour. Resist him, steadfast in faith, knowing that your fellow believers throughout the world undergo the same sufferings" (5:8–9). Or, it could also simply be that she has not done laundry in a while.

You might ask, "What's up with the T-shirt?" Sometimes people, or their clothing, say something that they really do not mean. Sometimes they mean just what they say, and their conclusions, ideas, or opinions let us know quickly that we may not be compatible or may have entirely different agendas.

Sometimes I don't feel like having sex, and then my husband beats me up. What should I do?

Your husband's views of sex and of how to build a loving relationship are both seriously out of whack. You should seek counseling as a couple or individually. If you feel that you are in danger, you should go now to a safe place.

Be aware that safe places do not necessarily include a parent's or a best friend's or a sister's house half a mile away. Possibilities include the diocesan family ministry office or a local domestic violence network, both to be found via the Internet, in the Yellow Pages, or perhaps through the local library. Google "safe place for women" and you'll find not just definitions and programs, but local places to go to.

Two handsome men live across the hall from me in a two-bedroom apartment. They are buff and they are snappy dressers, though one of them favors pink and uses, in my opinion, too much product in his fabulous hair. I suspect that they may be homosexual. What should I do?

Bring them a plate of brownies and say, "Welcome to the neighborhood." Unless the taste police task force of your building's homeowners association has strict strictures about hairdos and shirt colors, you should probably refrain from mentioning your own sartorial preferences in the beginning. And if one of them asks, "Do these jeans make me look fat?" the appropriate answer is always, "Not at all."

But I have some concerns about whether they use both bedrooms for sleeping or if one might be a den. Now what should I do?

Bring them a plate of brownies and say, "Welcome to the neighborhood." This may surprise you, but if your neighbors are not building a meth lab, constructing a hydroponic marijuana farm that compromises the building's structure, or engaging in a public display of law breaking that threatens the neighborhood, then how they employ their bedrooms is not your business and should not be your concern. Even if you suspect that they use both bedrooms so that they can quietly commit adultery with your straight neighbors, your intervention would be unwelcome and not at all neighborly. And you may be entirely incorrect about what is happening behind their closed doors.

Your own morality is not at risk here, unless you rush into judgment in such a way as to threaten your own salvation. Attend to the call of Jesus: "Stop judging, that you may not be judged. For as you judge, so will you be judged, and the measure with which you measure will be measured out to you" (Matt 7:1–2).

I am gay and live with my partner. Next door to us is a lesbian couple. We four are pretty happy. But across the hall is a young heterosexual couple. They fight a lot and loudly. If their marriage fails, will it be the fault of my partner and me, or of the two lesbians?

You and the lesbians are in the clear on this one. When marriages fail, it is usually the fault of the couples themselves. You should, however, continue to be good examples of serenity, purposeful dialogue, charitable conversation, and respect for neighbors who may have values different from your own.

If the turbulent young couple is new to your building, you might bring them a plate of brownies and say, "Welcome to the neighborhood." If they are not new to the building, you might bring them a plate of brownies and say simply, "I thought you might like to share the brownies I have just baked."

I do not know any gay couples. Is this my fault?

It may be that you are not paying attention. But you should be aware that gay people are not required to wear either badge or uniform. You may know any number of people whose orientation is homosexual: your dentist, bus driver, produce delivery person, or the person with whom you exchanged the kiss of peace at Mass last Sunday. Some of them may be vowed celibate. Others single. Some may have partners. Some may be sinners, and some may be saints.

When the bishop came to visit the confirmation class, my son raised his hand and asked, "Are you gay or straight?" The bishop look embarrassed, the pastor was outraged, the director of religious education was stunned, and the classroom teacher was mortified. Am I alone in thinking, "What's the matter with a little openness?"

No, you are not alone in your wonderment. Apparently your son agrees with your take, and he must have learned from you what back in the day we called "impertinence."

It is possible that you may be the only two who think that the kid's query was either well placed or well timed. If the bishop had a revelation to make about his sexual orientation, he might not feel that a visit with a class of high schoolers would be the moment to announce it. And how much would you worry about any adult who would choose to discuss such things with young students seeking confirmation? What you describe is not openness. The question your son asked was not phrased in a way to encourage openness. It seemed confrontational. And what's up with that? Perhaps you and your son could work together at coming up with alternative ways to question the bishop that would seem less designed to be provocative and more inclined toward inviting an exchange of information.

Reading your question makes me sad that the Wendy Ward School of Charm is no longer in business. No doubt both you and your son could have profited by studying there.

I am a gay man and want to marry my partner. Why is that not possible in today's Church?

There are and have always been other relationships and family structures in which God is honored and humankind is sanctified, but the Church reserves the term *marriage* for the unique relationship that includes not just the love between a man and a woman, but also the possibility of procreation. The primacy of marriage and its promise of procreation is explained even in the consecration of virgins when the bishop prays: "[God,] among your many gifts / you give to some the grace of virginity. / Yet the honor of marriage is in no way lessened. / As it was in the beginning, / your first blessing still remains upon this holy union."[17]

The marriage of a man and a woman is unique because of its synergistic effect, the whole (nuclear family with sons and daughters) being greater than the sum of its parts (the husband and wife). Thus, the Church reserves its first blessing for marriages. Should other unions that may have the potential of being demonstrably holy also be blessed or somehow recognized? Thoughtful souls will say that this conversation is today incomplete, even as the Church teaches that marriage has its origin in God's plan for humankind.

---

17. http://www.consecratedvirgins.org/rite.pdf, 7.

Then what about civil unions? A registered civil union is a legal relationship, but it isn't considered marriage. (It also isn't available in all fifty states.) What does the Church have to say about that?

A civil government may well decide to approve or license partnerships other than marriage. This would not change a Catholic theology of either marriage or sexuality.

Marriage has a tremendous tax benefit (filing jointly, for example); why shouldn't gay couples in a civil union have the same benefit? Should tax law really depend on sexual preference?

The issue to which you point is certainly one that civil legislatures may well deal with, as it seems to relate to both civil rights and matters of social justice. But the issue you raise is not one that is answered by a Catholic theology of marriage or of sexuality.

I know of a company that provides health-insurance benefits to spouses but not to partners in registered civil unions, whether they are a gay or a heterosexual couple. Is this fair? Is it just?

Surely no Catholic person would want anyone to be deprived of health care or insurance benefits. How to approach these matters is a great concern for all people of good will. A commitment to justice and the dignity of all God's people suggests that the matter to which you point be explored openly and honestly. But the issue is not one that is answered by a Catholic theology of marriage or of sexuality.

As a Catholic, am I obliged to be against any effort to recognize same-sex partnerships, or any corporate effort to provide benefits to such couples?

Since no Catholic person would want anyone to be deprived of health care or insurance benefits, it would seem that you should encourage open conversation about matters of justice. But work to be clear about which issues are answered by a Catholic theology of marriage or of sexuality and which are not.

A civil government or a corporation may well decide to make certain benefits available to households that do not include sacramental marriages. Catholic people should not regard such efforts as a commentary on or critique of the sacrament of marriage, but as an effort to secure justice for all God's people.

Keep in mind the Church's teaching that marriage is an institution ordained and blessed by God. If we truly believe this teaching, we should not worry that any human effort, legislation, or sin will scuttle what God has designed.

What about hospital visitation? I have heard a politician say that if gay couples can visit each other in the hospital, Christian marriage is at risk. How can this be?

We normally do not depend on politicians to teach moral theology or ethics, though we do expect them to demonstrate what goodness and justice look like in person, in policy, and in law. The politician to whom you refer should never be permitted to teach logic. When you or your spouse are in the hospital's intensive care unit, the exact nature of the relationship between the person in the next bed and her visitor is likely not to be among your most pressing concerns. Even if they are sinful in ways that are difficult to imagine, it is more difficult to imagine how their sinfulness might capsize your marriage.

Okay, maybe this is not really a question about sex. But I think that it is. My wife and I are divorced. She is seeking an annulment from the Church. But we have two children. I have heard that if we are annulled, the children will be both illegitimate and bastards. Is this fair?

A marriage that has ended in a civil divorce may, at the request of one or other of the concerned parties, be judged by the Church to be null, which is to say that it lacked a sacramental character. Your children were born of a civil marriage, and they are not at all at issue when a decree of nullity is issued. And, by the way, the marriage would be declared null, not you. Or the kids.

Do you find it interesting that critics of the Church or of annulments only refer to children as bastards or as illegitimate after an annulment, not after a divorce and not when born out of wedlock? What's up with that, do you think?

Did those famous lovers Abelard and Heloise really end up, one a monk without genitalia and the other a nun in a convent?

Yes. Theirs is a love story marked by tragedy. In the twelfth century, Peter Abelard was a French philosopher and teacher. His love affair with Heloise changed their lives in dramatic ways. She was homeschooled by her uncle in Paris until Abelard moved into the house to complete Heloise's education. She was twenty years younger, but they became lovers and had a son. At some point, Heloise and Abelard married secretly. With their son, they left the uncle's home. Heloise went to stay in a convent temporarily; her uncle and family believed Abelard had abandoned her, and they forced her to become a nun. Later, the uncle attacked and castrated Abelard, who then also went off and entered a monastery. The two former lovers carried on a famous correspondence that is filled with passion.

Theirs is an interesting story, but why did you ask?

Given the Abelard and Heloise story, can I presume that convents and monasteries are filled with sexual cripples?

No. Such a presumption would be erroneous. But as we consider the story, the convent and the monastery seem to be places of refuge for sinners or victims, not harbors of sexual dysfunction, don't you think?

Just as a woman and a man must each freely commit her- or himself to marriage or there can be no marriage, so also must monks and nuns seek to enter a monastery of their own free will and at the monastic community's invitation. In fact, St. Benedict, in his *Rule for Monasteries*, suggests that the aspirant must knock three times in order to gain entry to test his religious vocation. No one is or could be forced to enter in the current age. And while the occasional sexually unhealthy person may be found in a monastery or convent—as such a person may be found anywhere else—this has been proven to be far more the exception than the rule.

Today, all those who seek to enter religious life as priests, monks, brothers, sisters, or nuns undergo counseling and screening so that good health may prevail in individuals and groups, and in all the Church.

VIII

ISSUES RELATIVE
TO TECHNOLOGY

What about artificial insemination? Isn't the Church behind the times in not supporting such an advance?

Because something is technologically possible is no guarantee that it is either a good idea or in keeping with human dignity. It is unlikely that all the ramifications and implications of the developing science of artificial insemination are clearly understood. The Church's cautious teaching that children be conceived naturally should be widely appreciated as conserving human dignity, the rightful place of sexual activity in relationships, and the proper relationship of man and woman. Those who believe that it is their right to have children by any means possible may find this approach disheartening, but we are reminded that having children is not a right, but rather a privilege and a gift. Sometimes, through no fault of their own, couples are not given this gift.

What about if ours is a test-tube or petri-dish baby? If it is my egg and if the sperm comes from my husband, does that change things at all?

No; whence come the sperm and egg does not change how the matter is viewed. Perhaps you thought you'd not live long enough to hear Rome come down unequivocally on the side of sexual activity, but here you have it. Children are viewed by the Church as a gift of God given when a husband and wife, through the mutual gift of themselves, develop a union of two persons in which they seek to perfect one another and cooperate with God in the generation and rearing of new lives.

So, married love may go beyond the loving interchange of husband and wife in bringing new life into being. Thus, married love includes conjugal love. This theology of Christian marital practice sees nature as part of God's plan, thus excluding considerations of petri dishes, test tubes, or other technological assists.

I know a single mother who was impregnated by artificial insemination. I have told my pastor that he cannot baptize that child. He laughed at me. To whom shall I write about that outrage—the pope or one of his deputies?

Parents and godparents who present children for baptism are told as the baptismal ritual unfolds, "You must make it your constant care to bring them up in the practice of the faith." The parents and godparents then renew the vows of their own baptism. After that, they are asked, "Is it your will" that your children "should be baptized in the faith of the Church which we have professed with you?" If they answer, "It is," the baptism proceeds.

They are not asked, "Tell us of the circumstances in which this child was conceived." Would a child conceived during rape be baptized? Of course. The child of parents who no longer love each other? Certainly. One of the wonderful attributes of the Church is that she welcomes and embraces in baptism all God's children who come to the waters.

Back when some cultures considered women somehow less than fully human, the Church gave its considered judgment of such foolishness by baptizing girls and women without comment or discussion. This is a proud piece of our Christian heritage.

There may be some parents who are sinful. Others may have conceived children in ways that are immoral or irregular. This has no bearing on the need of the children to be loved and welcomed by the Church in the saving waters.

The pope, the cardinals and bishops, and all the Church's teachers necessarily endorse this constant practice of the Church. If you do not, you would be wise not to tell them, unless you mention it to your confessor; keep it a secret from the others until your heart is changed by prayer and good works to be a bit more like the heart of Jesus.

My daughter was asked to be a surrogate mother, to carry a fetus for a woman who has had a history of miscarriages. My daughter insists that to be of service to a couple in such a way is the "Christian Thing" to do. Is it?

It can be burdensome when folks suggest that what they want to do or what they somehow interpret as nice is the "Christian Thing" to do. Perhaps your daughter does view such service as a kindness, but as it is not in keeping with Church teaching, she'd find few theologians or pastors who would agree with her assessment. She might examine news reports of other surrogates and their services and the unimaginable consequences, conflicts, lawsuits, confusions, and difficulties that can arise—unimaginable, that is, until they do arise. It is difficult to be gentle with people (though we must) who make decisions that conflict with Church teachings and practices, then seek affirmation from the

Church in their choice, and are annoyed or combative when a contrary point is raised. Some of us consider such people among the poor we will always have with us.

Why does the Church consider it wrong to be sterilized, to have tubes tied, or to have a vasectomy? Shouldn't this be a private matter?

The Church can help us understand matters that might seem private. To seek medical assistance in a way that not only prevents pregnancy but also changes or even mutilates the body may well not be in keeping with human dignity. Such a procedure may be medically necessary in some situations. When it is not a medical necessity, one must carefully examine motive and desire and seek to burnish her or his opinion against the Church's teaching about the purposes of sexuality, human dignity, and the sanctity of the human body.

And what about cloning? Why can't there be two or three of me?

Cloning is a science that is in its infancy. No good case has been made showing it to be in keeping with an informed view of human dignity.

What is the difference, in terms of morality, between being a blood donor and a sperm donor? Life-giving fluid is life-giving fluid, right?

Perhaps it would be helpful to make a distinction: blood sustains life while sperm transmits life. The Church approves of donating blood. It may well be the "Christian Thing" to do. Donating sperm, on the other hand, is contrary to the Church's moral teaching on the proper use of sex.

My boyfriend was a sperm donor as a college student and, for all I know, could have a dozen children he has never met. I told him that I am afraid that one of our future children could meet and marry a half sibling. He says, "Oh, grow up," and, "That could never happen." Could it? Am I wrong to feel unsettled about his contributions to building a more populous world?

You sound pretty grown up. Your concerns sound both real and serious. The burden of proof is on your boyfriend. Have him visit the clinic where he made either his donations or his sales and learn from them how many children he has. And where they live. And if they have expressed a wish to know their biological father. He might also ask the clinic to share with him the procedures in place to see that siblings not meet and fall in love. The fact that there could be so many complications that might affect so many people suggests a very certain wisdom in the Church's call to caution.

IX

PHILOSOPHICAL QUERIES

Why do so few folks look to the Church for guidance on sexual matters?

We live in an age that attaches a high value to the individual, and the individual to her or his opinion. It is a sadness that so many seem to regard their opinions as nearly the equivalent of divine revelation. When we prize our own thoughts above all others, we are not true persons of dialogue, and we are not good learners. Even though the Church is composed of sinners, surely there is greater wisdom in the deliberations and the constant prayer and study of Scripture by a large group, Christ's own Body, guided by the Holy Spirit, than any one of us can produce on our own. To be part of a Church and to be a lifelong learner may seem unfashionable to some. Holy, whole people seek wisdom where wisdom can be found.

Why does the Catholic Church care—or have anything to say—about sex? And, more specifically, why does a group of old, celibate men have the right or wisdom to address the issue at all?

If one wishes to discount the Church's wisdom, she or he can characterize the Church as no more than a group of old and celibate men wandering aimlessly around the marble palaces of the Vatican, issuing commands about things they do not understand. If one wishes to understand her- or himself in the context of what it means to be fully human on a path from here to eternity, she or he will look for wisdom where it can be found. Clearly, all of the Church's great thinkers and extraordinary resources, not to mention divine guidance, employed over the course of millennia, bring greater experience and wisdom to our considerations than even the brightest of young adults can accomplish alone or with a couple of hours devoted to cruising the Internet. To admit this, though, requires a very certain humility.

The Church cares about sex because our attitudes about it and the ways in which we employ our sexuality will either send us to God or shroud his goodness and maybe even damn us. Sex is God's gift to populate the earth and give pleasure to humankind as holy relationships, reflective of God's glory, are built and sustained. This is both why the Church cares and why the Church has lots to say.

Can we separate a consideration of sex and sexuality from our Catholic life of sacraments?

We cannot. St. Irenaeus of Lyons, an early Church father and a doctor of the Church, writing in the last quarter of the second century in what is now France, reminded us that we are members of the Body of Christ and are nourished by God's creation, the God who causes the sun to rise and the rain to fall. St. Irenaeus also notes that "when the chalice we mix and the bread we bake receive the word of God, the eucharistic elements become the body and blood of Christ by which our bodies live and grow. How then can it be said that the flesh belonging to the Lord's own body and nourished by his body and blood is incapable of receiving God's gift of eternal life?"[18] We receive growth from that which we are given as gift.

And to what end is our growth? St. Basil the Great, writing in the fourth century, tells us that "through the Spirit we acquire a likeness to God; indeed, we attain what is beyond our most sublime aspirations—we become God."[19] We return to our great confidence in asking God to "love in us / what you loved in your Son" (Preface for Sundays in Ordinary Time VII). And so we ask that we might "come to share in the divinity of Christ, who humbled himself to share in our humanity" (the prayer of the priest as water is added to the wine at the preparation of the gifts).

The message seems to be that as we struggle to understand sex and sexuality, we should stick close to the Lord's table where we will be nourished and sustained as we continue the trek, seeking God in the details and even in the messiness of our lives.

What if the Church says A, but I do B? Can I still be a good Catholic?

It depends. We must begin any consideration not with our own opinion, but with a clear understanding of what is truly at issue in the matter under consideration. We should be clear about what the Church teaches and why. If one does not immediately understand the wisdom of a position or teaching, one should not understand this to mean that the Church is wrong and should change to share our more

---

18. From Irenaeus of Lyons, *Against Heresies*, written about AD 185 (Lib. 5, 2, 2–3; SC 153, 30–38).

19. Basil the Great, from the treatise *On the Holy Spirit*, http://www-st-philip.net/presentations/On_the_Holy-Spirit.pdf.

enlightened approach. Be well aware that some teachings are difficult, not so much difficult to understand as hard to put into practice.

She or he who does B when the Church teaches A might be poorly informed, confused, sinful, or oblivious. The Church does not require that we know every facet of every teaching, but rather that we seek to conform ourselves to the ideal, and the ideal is Jesus. When we understand that this is the true end of all Church teaching, we seek a better understanding with a more supple heart.

My professor tells me that *his* professor told him never to talk about sex. What did he mean?

As the dialogue in this book has suggested, seeking to discuss or understand matters relating to sexuality can be fraught with tension and can create moments ripe for misunderstanding. As we approach the discussion with open minds and hearts, we should feel comforted by the guiding presence of the Spirit of Jesus, who reminds us what we hear many, many times in the Scriptures but are too quick to forget or disregard: "Do not be afraid" (Matt 14:27).

All I know about *Humanae Vitae* is that the name is in Latin and that it says, "No!" to birth control. Did the pope have something else going on there?

Yes, there is a lot going on in *On Human Life*, the English title of Pope Paul VI's final encyclical. It is an extraordinary document that explains and celebrates the dignity of Christian marriage. Take a look:

Married love particularly reveals its true nature and nobility when we realize that it takes its origin from God, who "is love," the Father "from whom every family in heaven and on earth is named."

[And:] Marriage...is in reality the wise and provident institution of God the Creator, whose purpose was to effect in man His loving design. As a consequence, husband and wife, through that mutual gift of themselves, which is specific and exclusive to them alone, develop that union of two persons in which they perfect one another, cooperating with God in the generation and rearing of new lives.

The marriage of those who have been baptized is, in addition, invested with the dignity of a sacramental sign of grace, for it represents the union of Christ and His Church....

[Further, married love is then] an act of the free will, whose trust is such that it is meant not only to survive the joys and sorrows of daily life, but also to grow, so that husband and wife become in a way one heart and one soul, and together attain their human fulfillment....

[Finally:] this love...is not confined wholly to the loving interchange of husband and wife; it also contrives to go beyond this to bring new life into being. "Marriage and conjugal love are by their nature ordained toward the procreation and education of children. Children are really the supreme gift of marriage and contribute in the highest degree to their parents' welfare." (*HV* 8, 9)[20]

20. Paul VI, Humanae Vitae, http://www.vatican.va/holy_father/paul_vi/encyclicals/documents/hf_p-vi_enc_25071968_humanae-vitae_en.html. Quotations within the quotations are in the original encyclical and refer to Scripture verses and other Church documents.

Does anyone really care about the historical context of *Humanae Vitae*? Should they?

The historical context may interest you. Pope Paul VI was reported to have concerns about what was then called a "contraceptive mentality." The fear was that with the easy availability of reliable, artificial means of birth control, people might regard as separate the two purposes of marriage, the unitive and the procreative. That insight seems to have been prophetic as many people now appear to consider marriage a partnership that need not necessarily include openness to the possibility of giving birth to and raising children. The Church does not regard such a partnership as a sacramental marriage. Remember, one of the questions asked of prospective brides and grooms, a question that they answer publicly in the wedding ceremony, is, "Will you accept children lovingly from God and bring them up according to the law of Christ and the Church?"

We may be living in a culture with a definition of marriage that is different from the Church's, a change that was made possible when birth-control methods became both more reliable and easily accessible. The full implications of this cultural shift, clearly, are not yet known or fully apparent. Thus, ongoing dialogue, in a spirit of justice and charity, is both necessary and important, not to mention interesting. Stay tuned.

What about dissent? Is that a theological category?

Real dissent is not so common as one might think. The number of people who assert that the Church is wrong and they are correct is very small. Martin Luther, for example, is famously reported to have said, "Here I stand; I can do no other." He was a true dissenter.

Sometimes folks will hear a Church teaching or be vaguely aware of some facet of a teaching and say, "Well, I disagree." That is not dissent. Whether or not we understand, agree with, or put into practice a particular teaching is not a measure of the truth or beauty of the teaching.

Church teaching grows out of the reading of Scripture, out of prayer and study, and out of the lived experience of generations who have gone before us. When we find a particular teaching problematic in our own lives, the Church invites us to careful reflection on all the issues involved—and reminds us, of course, of the necessity of following our well-formed consciences.

What, in the end, ought to be the final word on how I understand and exercise my human sexuality? And will I have the final word, or might it belong to Jesus?

Do your best, keep your eyes on the prize, be attentive to others, and you will surely hear the voice of Jesus: "Come, you who are blessed by my Father. Inherit the kingdom prepared for you from the foundation of the world" (Matt 25:34).

So, we should be on the move to accomplish this just as Jesus, who gets the final word, advises: "Get up, let us go" (John 14:31).

X

TAKE IT TO THE LORD
IN PRAYER

*All of us, gazing with unveiled face on the glory
of the Lord,
are being transformed into the same image from
glory to glory.*

• 2 Corinthians 3:18

If we are to understand that in our sexuality we can commune with the love and mystery of God, shouldn't we take it to the Lord in prayer? But what would be the "it" that we take? Could it include our confusion and distress, as well as our hopes and our dreams?

Excellent point! Consider the answer to your fine query in this Prayer over the Gifts for the Fifth Sunday of Easter: "Lord God, / by this holy exchange of gifts / you share with us your divine life. / Grant that everything we do / may be directed by the knowledge of your truth." Cool that so much of what the Church teaches is first and best explained in the Church's prayer, don't you think? This fact makes one glad to belong to such a grand tradition.

Consider again the prayer above. It instructs us that God's truth is the answer to our confusion, the relief for our distress, the foundation of our hopes, and the realization of our dreams. So, all of our glory and our sorrow we take to God in prayer both in words and in silence.

How do we come to this knowledge of God's truth that is to be our guide? The prayers of the Church ought to help make our hearts and minds fertile ground so that we can attend to the truth of Scripture, ponder the teachings of our prayers, and consider the wisdom of the Church's tradition and teaching. With the Scriptures in one hand, the prayers of the Church in the other, and *The New York Times* within reach,[21] we can form our consciences so that they resonate with the challenges of God. In this way, we will find the truth, the truth that is revealed to reside in Jesus, who tells us, "I am the way and the truth and the life" (John 14:6). Jesus says more: "If you remain in my word, you will truly be my disciples, and you will know the truth, and the truth will set you free" (8:31–32). Surely this is good news for all seekers!

Okay, but I am not a priest or a theologian. Where shall I start?

Below, you'll find some of the Church's traditional prayers. Make them your own!

---

21. Karl Barth, considered by many to be one of the most important Christian thinkers of the twentieth century, is credited with advising that preachers go about their task with the Bible in one hand and *The New York Times* in the other. Barth means to suggest that current events call us to a new and special attentiveness to the Word of God as we craft our prayers and consider our concerns.

Traditional Catholic Prayers

The Lord's Prayer

> Our Father,
> who art in heaven,
> hallowed be thy name.
> Thy kingdom come.
> Thy will be done
> on earth as it is in heaven.
> Give us this day our daily bread,
> and forgive us our trespasses
> as we forgive those who trespass against us;
> and lead us not into temptation
> but deliver us from evil.
> Amen.

The Hail Mary

> Hail Mary, full of grace,
> the Lord is with thee.
> Blessed art thou among women
> and blessed is the fruit of thy womb, Jesus.
>
> Holy Mary, Mother of God,
> pray for us sinners, now
> and at the hour of our death.
> Amen.

The Glory Be (also known as the Doxology)

> Glory be to the Father
> and to the Son
> and to the Holy Spirit.
> As it was in the beginning,

is now, and ever shall be,
world without end.
Amen.

An Act of Contrition

O my God,
I am heartily sorry for having offended thee,
and I detest all my sins,
because I dread the loss of heaven and the pains of hell;
but most of all because they offend thee, my God,
who are all good and deserving of all my love.
I firmly resolve,
with the help of thy grace,
to confess my sins,
to do penance,
and to amend my life.
Amen.

An Act of Faith

O my God, I firmly believe
that you are one God in three divine Persons,
Father, Son, and Holy Spirit.
I believe that your divine Son became man
and died for our sins and that he will come
to judge the living and the dead.
I believe these and all the truths
which the Holy Catholic Church teaches
because you have revealed them,
who are eternal truth and wisdom,
who can neither deceive nor be deceived.
In this faith I intend to live and die.
Amen.

An Act of Hope

O Lord God,
I hope by your grace for the pardon of all my sins,
and after life here to gain eternal happiness
because you have promised it,
who are infinitely powerful, faithful, kind, and
    merciful.
In this hope I intend to live and die.
Amen.

An Act of Love

O Lord God, I love you above all things
and I love my neighbor for your sake
because you are the highest, infinite, and perfect
    good,
worthy of all my love.
In this love I intend to live and die.
Amen.

St. Francis of Assisi's Prayer before the Crucifix

Most High, glorious God,
enlighten the darkness of my heart.
Give me true faith,
certain hope, and perfect charity,
sense, and knowledge, Lord,
that I may carry out
your holy and true command.

Prayer of St. Thomas Aquinas, i

Grant, O Merciful God,
that I may ardently desire,

prudently examine,
truthfully acknowledge,
and perfectly accomplish
what is pleasing to you,
for the praise and glory of your name!

Prayer of St. Thomas Aquinas, ii

Grant, O merciful God, that I may ardently desire,
carefully examine, truly know, and perfectly fulfill
those things that are pleasing to you
and to the praise and glory of your holy name.
Direct my life, O my God,
and grant that I might know what you would have
    me to do
and for me to fulfill it as is necessary and profitable
    to my soul.
Grant to me, O Lord my God,
that I may not be found wanting in prosperity or in
    adversity
and that I may not be lifted up by one nor cast down
    by the other.
May I find joy in nothing but what leads to you
and sorrow in nothing but what leads away from
    you.
May I seek to please no one or fear to displease
    anyone save only you.
Grant to me, O Lord God, a vigilant heart
that no subtle speculation may ever lead me from
    you;
a noble heart that no unworthy affection may draw
    me from you;
an upright heart that no evil purpose may turn me
    from you.

Give me a steadfast heart that no tribulation may
shatter
and a free heart that no violent affection may claim
as its own.
And finally, grant me, O Lord my God, a mind to
know you,
diligence to seek you, wisdom to find you.
Give me a way of life pleasing to you;
perseverance to trust and await you in confidence
that I shall embrace you at the last.
Amen.

Prayer attributed to St. Benedict

O gracious and holy Father,
give us wisdom to perceive you,
intelligence to understand you,
diligence to seek you,
eyes to behold you,
a heart to meditate upon you,
and a life to proclaim you,
through the power of the Spirit
of Jesus Christ our Lord.

St. Patrick's Breastplate

So stand fast with your loins girded in truth,
clothed with righteousness as a breastplate.
• Ephesians 6:14

I bind unto myself today
The strong Name of the Trinity,
By invocation of the same,
The Three in One and One in Three.

Christ be with me, Christ within me,
Christ behind me, Christ before me,
Christ beside me, Christ to win me,
Christ to comfort and restore me.
Christ beneath me, Christ above me,
Christ in quiet, Christ in danger,
Christ in hearts of all that love me,
Christ in mouth of friend and stranger.

I bind unto myself the Name,
The strong Name of the Trinity;
By invocation of the same.
The Three in One, and One in Three,
Of whom all nature hath creation,
Eternal Father, Spirit, Word:
Praise to the Lord of my salvation,
Salvation is of Christ the Lord.

You suggest seeking to make our hearts like the heart of Jesus. What might such a heart look like?

Pope St. Leo the Great, who reigned from 440 to 461, observed that whatever was visible in Christ has passed over into the sacraments. And here is what was visible in Christ: inclusion for the isolated, healing for the sick, light for those in darkness, food for the hungry, drink for the thirsty, balm for the afflicted, sight for the blind, and new life for the dead. In praying the litany below, meditate on the heart of Jesus and the love poured out from it. Then listen for the voice of Jesus calling you to "go and do likewise" (Luke 10:37).

Litany of the Sacred Heart of Jesus
(revised and abridged)

> Lord, have mercy.
> *Christ, have mercy.*
> Lord, have mercy.
> *Christ, graciously hear us.*
>
> God, the Father of Heaven, *have mercy on us.*
> God, the Son, Redeemer of the world, *have mercy on us.*
> God, the Holy Spirit, *have mercy on us.*
> Holy Trinity, one God, *have mercy on us.*
> Heart of Jesus, Son of the Eternal Father, *have mercy on us.*
> Heart of Jesus, formed in the womb of the Virgin Mother by the Holy Spirit, *have mercy on us.*
> Heart of Jesus, one with the Word of God, *have mercy on us.*
> Heart of Jesus, house of God and gate of heaven, *have mercy on us.*
> Heart of Jesus, glowing in charity, *have mercy on us.*
> Heart of Jesus, vessel of justice and love, *have mercy on us.*
> Heart of Jesus, center of all hearts, *have mercy on us.*
> Heart of Jesus, in whom are all the treasures of wisdom and knowledge, *have mercy on us.*
> Heart of Jesus, of whose fullness we have all received, *have mercy on us.*
> Heart of Jesus, patient and rich in mercy, *have mercy on us.*
> Heart of Jesus, crushed for our iniquities, *have mercy on us.*
> Heart of Jesus, made obedient unto death, *have mercy on us.*

Heart of Jesus, pierced with a lance, *have mercy on us.*

Heart of Jesus, source of all consolation, *have mercy on us.*

Heart of Jesus, our life and resurrection, *have mercy on us.*

Heart of Jesus, our peace and reconciliation, *have mercy on us.*

Heart of Jesus, salvation of those who hope in you, *have mercy on us.*

Heart of Jesus, delight of all saints, *have mercy on us.*

Lamb of God, who takes away the sins of the world, *spare us, O Lord.*

Lamb of God, who takes away the sins of the world, *graciously hear us, O Lord.*

Lamb of God, who takes away the sins of the world, *have mercy on us.*

V. Jesus, meek and humble of Heart,
R. Conform our hearts to be like yours.

Let us pray:
Almighty and everlasting God,
look upon the Heart of your Son
and in your great goodness, grant pardon to all who
   seek your mercy,
in the name of the same Jesus Christ, your Son,
who lives and reigns with you and the Holy Spirit,
world without end.
Amen.

Why are the psalms so often called the "Church's Prayer Book"?

The psalms are poems and songs, some composed by King David, who danced before the Ark of God, written and sung to celebrate every human emotion. They tell the stories of God's power and mercy and invite us to bring our days and deeds before God in praise and thanksgiving. The psalms are used in the Liturgy of the Hours each day throughout the world.

All 150 psalms can be found online through the generosity of the United States Conference of Catholic Bishops: http://www.usccb.org/nab/bible/index.shtml#psalms. This link is for *The New American Bible*, which is the standard Catholic translation.

Additionally, the New Revised Standard Version Bible is also available online, courtesy of the Division of Christian Education of the National Council of the Churches of Christ in the United States of America: http://www.devotions.net/bible/00bible.htm; the psalms are: http://www.devotions.net/bible/00old.htm.

You might consider using the following as morning prayer: Psalm 1, 2, 63, or 149. In the evening or at night: Psalm 141, 142, 110, or 114.

Here are two of the most popular of the psalms; taken from the New Revised Standard Version:

Psalm 23

A Psalm of David

> The LORD is my shepherd, I shall not want.
>   He makes me lie down in green pastures;
> he leads me beside still waters;
>   he restores my soul.

He leads me in right paths
    for his name's sake.

Even though I walk through the darkest valley,
    I fear no evil;
for you are with me;
    your rod and your staff—
    they comfort me.

You prepare a table before me
    in the presence of my enemies;
you anoint my head with oil;
    my cup overflows.
Surely goodness and mercy shall follow me
    all the days of my life,
and I shall dwell in the house of the LORD
    my whole life long.

Psalm 51

Prayer for Cleansing and Pardon
A Psalm of David

Have mercy on me, O God,
    according to your steadfast love;
according to your abundant mercy
    blot out my transgressions.
Wash me thoroughly from my iniquity,
    and cleanse me from my sin.

For I know my transgressions,
    and my sin is ever before me.
Against you, you alone, have I sinned,
    and done what is evil in your sight,

so that you are justified in your sentence
   and blameless when you pass judgment.
Indeed, I was born guilty,
   a sinner when my mother conceived me.

You desire truth in the inward being;
   therefore teach me wisdom in my secret heart.
Purge me with hyssop, and I shall be clean;
   wash me, and I shall be whiter than snow.
Let me hear joy and gladness;
   let the bones that you have crushed rejoice.
Hide your face from my sins,
   and blot out all my iniquities.

Create in me a clean heart, O God,
   and put a new and right spirit within me.
Do not cast me away from your presence,
   and do not take your holy spirit from me.
Restore to me the joy of your salvation,
   and sustain in me a willing spirit.

Then I will teach transgressors your ways,
   and sinners will return to you.
Deliver me from bloodshed, O God,
      O God of my salvation,
      and my tongue will sing aloud of your deliverance.

O LORD, open my lips,
   and my mouth will declare your praise.
For you have no delight in sacrifice;
   if I were to give a burnt offering, you would not
      be pleased.

The sacrifice acceptable to God is a broken spirit;
    a broken and contrite heart, O God, you will
        not despise.

Do good to Zion in your good pleasure;
    rebuild the walls of Jerusalem,
then you will delight in right sacrifices,
    in burnt offerings and whole burnt offerings;
    then bulls will be offered on your altar.

Well, all those prayers are swell, and I want to make them my own so that, as St. Paul advised, I can "pray without ceasing" (1 Thess 5:17). But can I also say prayers that I myself compose? I know my needs, I think, and want to bring them to God. How can I start?

Wonderful plan. Of course, you can frame your own prayers. You'll find below some examples that might serve as a model for you, then go to it!

The United States Conference of Catholic Bishops provides an enormously helpful Web site (http://www.usccb.org) that features the Scripture readings and psalm for every day of the year, as well as the complete text of *The New American Bible*. This is a rich source for prayerful inspiration. The examples of reflections and prayers inspired by the daily Scriptures below are offered with the hope that the reader will make daily use of Scripture in crafting personal prayers to God in supplication, praise, and thanksgiving.

Prayer Prompts and Examples

When I am not sure if I should remain in the Church

Reading I: Jonah 3:1–10
Gospel: Luke 11:29–32

Reflection

Who could be wiser than Solomon? In the proclamation of the Scriptures, there is a wisdom greater than Solomon's. Vatican II, in the "Constitution on the Sacred Liturgy," reminds us that Christ "is present in His word, since it is He Himself who speaks when the holy scriptures are read in the Church" (7). Here is a blessing and a burden for the reader who reads with the very voice of Christ.

And Jonah? He emerged from three days in the belly of a whale and was enormously successful as a prophet. Those who heard him turned their backs on wickedness and repented of their sins. But in the breaking of the bread, there is something, someone, greater than Jonah, for "Christ is always present in His Church, especially in her liturgical celebrations. He is present in the sacrifice of the Mass, not only in the person of His minister...but especially under the Eucharistic species." Christ is also present "when the Church prays and sings, for He promised: 'Where two or three are gathered together in my name, there am I in the midst of them' (Matt. 18:20)" (ibid.).

And, even with our troubled history and amidst the scandals that stain us, "the Church has never failed to come together to celebrate the paschal mystery" (ibid., 6). We are blessed to be in that faithful number.

Prayer

> Almighty God,
> you who plunge us into the paschal mystery by
>   baptism,
> keep us steadfast in the teaching of the apostles
> and in the communion of the breaking of the bread
> that the victory and triumph of the death and
>   resurrection
> be always present among us.
> We ask this through Christ,
> our deliverance and our hope,
> one with you and the Holy Spirit,
> forever and ever.

When I am a victim

Reading I: Daniel 13:1–9, 15–17, 19–30, 33–62
Gospel: John 8:1–11

Reflection

Susanna was a victim. The elders who saw her walking in the garden are described in one translation of the Book of Daniel as "perverted" men. They "suppressed their consciences; they would not allow their eyes to look to heaven, and did not keep just judgments." Susanna cried to God, and "the LORD heard her prayer." God then "stirred up the holy spirit of a young boy named Daniel," who told the sons of Israel that they had foolishly condemned a daughter of Israel "without examination and without clear evidence."

When the liars were convicted for bearing false witness, "the whole assembly cried aloud, blessing God who saves those who hope in him." And "innocent blood was saved that day."

Jesus, too, saves a woman. This one is apparently not innocent, but has been caught in the act of adultery. He rescues her from cruel execution by stoning. We are left to ponder how the woman alone was caught in the act of adultery. Adultery is not a solo sin; where was the man and why was he not brought for punishment by the scribes and Pharisees? We do not know what Jesus writes in the dust, but his charge to the crowd when he stands up and sends them away in embarrassed silence is stunning: "Let the one among you who is without sin be the first to throw a stone at her." They leave, beginning with the elders, who, we might think, ought to have known better to begin with.

Our caution today is the final message of Jesus to the woman: "Neither do I condemn you. Go, and from now on do not sin any more." Jesus calls us to repent of our own sins. We are also not to count the sins and failings of those we must seek to forgive. And as we seek to forgive, we are reminded of how richly we ourselves have been forgiven.

Prayer

Almighty God,
you who plunge us into the paschal mystery by
    baptism,
make us well aware of our sinfulness and frailty,
but even more, give us a growing consciousness
of your tender mercy to us
and to the whole people you seek to gather to
    yourself
in the coming feast of victory and triumph.
We ask this favor through Christ,
our deliverance and our hope,

one with you and the Holy Spirit,
forever and ever.

When I am in doubt or confused

Reading I: Numbers 21:4–9
Gospel: John 8:21–30

Reflection

In the Gospel, the Jews ask Christ a simple question, a question that Christians and nonbelievers are still asking two thousand years later: "Who are you?"

How difficult it is for Jesus to answer that simple question when his listeners are challenged by the limits of humanity. So he offers context that perhaps the Jews, the Pharisees, and modern Catholics can understand—an authority. If you ever had a substitute teacher, you know that the successful ones were able to convince you and your classmates that you were expected to parse all the nouns, conjugate all the verbs, clean all the chalkboards, and run twenty laps before lunch because your teacher said so. Even though Jesus is indeed the teacher, he invokes the authority of the Father: "I say only what the Father has taught me. The one who sent me is with me. He has not left me alone, because I always do what is pleasing to him."

Moses also acts as a spokesperson for the Lord—a task that Moses felt both unprepared for and unworthy to assume. And when God observed that the people of Israel were complaining to his faithful servant, he was not happy. He not only punished the whiners, he made sure that everyone in the class would remember what could happen to them if they followed suit.

And then came healing. Moses crafted "a bronze serpent and mounted it on a pole [this is the symbol medical doctors use today], and whenever anyone who had been bitten by a serpent looked at the bronze serpent, he lived."

Jesus, a good Jew who knew that story, tells us, "When you lift up the Son of Man [on the cross], then you will realize that I AM [the same name God told Moses when speaking from the burning bush]."

Whenever there is confusion or doubt as our imperfect ears and hearts struggle to understand his teachings, Jesus gently reminds us, "The one who sent me is true, and what I heard from him I tell the world."

John, the Gospel writer tells us, "Because he spoke this way, many came to believe in him." May we be forever in that number.

Prayer

> Good and gracious God:
> motherly in mercy and father-like in compassion,
> you gave your servant Moses wisdom and grace
> to recognize your authority
> and to trust in your plan for the deliverance of the
>   Israelites
> from sin and slavery into the land of your promise.
> Give us the faith we need to trust in you
> as we continue our pilgrimage
> enslaved by our doubt,
> but encouraged by the promise of deliverance from
>   our sins.
> We ask this through Jesus Christ, your Son, our Lord.

When I am about to make a promise

Reading I: Daniel 3:14–20, 91–92, 95
Reading II: Daniel 3:52–56
Gospel: John 8:31–42

Reflection

When we Christians renew our baptismal promises, we're asked, "Do you believe in the one true God? Do you believe in Jesus, who suffered, died, and was buried, and who rose from the dead?"

It is extraordinary even to our modern ears that a man could come back to life after the violent and merciless death that we will remember on Good Friday. But it was nearly as extraordinary for Old Testament folks to declare their faith in one God—not merely a supreme being above all other gods but the only God, the God of the First Commandment.

In the Book of Daniel, King Nebuchadnezzar wants to unify his kingdom of Babylon—a kingdom that includes Assyrians, Persians, Israelites, and many other groups. To that end, Nebuchadnezzar decides to make all of his people worship one god. And he will be that god. No matter who succeeds Nebuchadnezzar as king, Babylon will remain solid on the foundation of the common worship of the king. He builds a golden idol in his likeness and tries to convince people of influence among various ethnic groups to worship the idol. He offers a powerful incentive: bow down before the idol—and persuade your countrymen to do the same—or you will be put to death. Not many refuse.

Except three Israelites: Shadrach, Meshach, and Abednego. Their faith in the one, true God is so strong that they proclaim: "If our God can save us from the white-hot furnace and from your hands, O king, may he save us! But even if he will not, know, O king, that we will not serve your god or worship the golden statue that you set up."

This, of course, throws Nebuchadnezzar into a blind fury. He makes the fire seven times hotter, certain that the death of three young Israelites will not only seal their fate but also confirm his own status as a deity.

Imagine his surprise. The God of the Israelites does not merely spare Shadrach, Meshach, and Abednego from their trial by fire; he allows them to endure it and survive it. Even the mighty king of Babylon is humbled. He says, "Blessed be the God of Shadrach, Meshach, and Abednego."

We remember this as we continue our journey to share the passion and resurrection of Christ, who was not spared his trial, but suffered, died, and was glorified through resurrection in order to rescue us from sin. In the Gospel of John, Jesus reminds us, "If the Son frees you, then you will truly be free."

Let us continue life's journey secure in the faith that will come to perfection through the life, death, and resurrection of Jesus, our Christ and our brother.

Prayer

> Father in heaven,
> giver of all good gifts,
> you shower us with treasure.
> Give us also the wisdom and perseverance
> that we may know your Word, understand your will,
> and continue to do your work.
> In Christ's holy name we pray.

When I am in distress

Reading I: Jeremiah 20:10–13
Psalm: Psalm 18:2–3, 3–4, 5–6, 7
Gospel: John 10:31–42

Reflection

The refrain for the psalm above is the cry of one who seeks shelter in God from the storm: "In my distress I called upon the LORD, / and he heard my voice." The last verse exults: "From his temple he heard my voice, / and my cry to him reached his ears."

The prophet Jeremiah shares this confidence. He asserts that "the LORD is with me, like a mighty champion." He sees God's loyalty to him and to all the faithful, in a way that unsettles twenty-first-century Christians. He writes that "my persecutors will stumble, they will not triumph." Not only will they not triumph, but he asks God, "Let me witness the vengeance you take on them."

The prophet recalls God's goodness, God's faithfulness, God's justice. Is his cry for vengeance better understood as a petition that God's justice reign in every place and every heart? Human vengeance is clearly ruled out; we are not called to judge or to punish. We are called to seek both justice and truth and this, it seems, is what fuels the prophet's entreaties. He says to God, "to you I have entrusted my cause." If he is faithful to God who is first in faithfulness, then he will see justice: the wicked converted, and wickedness punished. Then goodness will reign. This vision prompts Jeremiah to conclude with praise: "Sing to the LORD, / praise the LORD, / For he has rescued the life of the poor / from the power of the wicked!"

We see in John's Gospel a reason we are not called to judge others: we could be just as incorrect as those who considered Jesus a blasphemer and who "reached for rocks to stone him." Jesus spoke to his accusers of his mission "as he whom the father consecrated and sent into the world." However, "at these words they again tried to arrest him, but he eluded their grasp."

How did he elude their grasp? We are not told. But they had clearly failed to grasp the import of what he told them. Others, however, across the Jordan, who heard him "came to believe in him."

May we be in the number of the believers who hear him, and may we seek to imitate him in our own search for wisdom and justice.

Prayer

> O God,
> rock, fortress, deliverer,
> be our shield against all wickedness
> in our own hearts and in the hearts of all your
>   people,
> that we who approach life's journey
> uplifted by our baptismal promises
> may be kept safe from all harm
> on the way to your house where you live and reign
> with Christ, through whom we make this prayer
> in the unity of the Holy Spirit,
> one God forever.

When I seek Christ in communion

Reading I: Acts 3:1–10
Gospel: Luke 24:13–35

Reflection

The road to Emmaus provides a model for the Church's liturgy: greeting, Liturgy of the Word, homily, table prayer, sharing of the blessed bread and wine, recognition of the Lord in our midst and at our table.

Why did the disciples not recognize him? Luke tells us, "Jesus himself drew near and walked with them, but their eyes were prevented from recognizing him." Luke might also provide a hint about why they did not recognize him; we see the hint in the verb tense: "We were hoping that he would be the one to redeem Israel." As they tell the story of Jesus and their hopes, they use the past tense. Their hope is gone. They report that "some women" from their group astounded them by reporting that they were at the tomb early in the morning but did not find his body; but they "reported that they had indeed seen a vision of angels who announced that he was alive." Others, presumably the men, went then to the tomb "and found things just as the women had described, but him they did not see."

The disciples learn, when they recognize Christ in the breaking of the bread, that the Church never speaks of the risen Lord in the past tense. When the liturgy was first translated into English, the first memorial acclamation was incorrectly rendered as "Christ has died, Christ has risen, Christ will come again." The "has risen" was quickly changed to the more accurate "is risen." This Christ is always present to the Church in the present tense and not just as a sweet memory.

Prayer

God of fulfilled promises and expectant dreams,
you nourish us in Word and Sacrament,

calling us to recognize you
in the broken bread of Scripture and Eucharist.
May our minds be supple and our hearts tender,
that we may always seek you and know you
in promises kept,
in broken bread,
and in your Church's communion.
Grant this favor through Christ our Lord.

When I see light

Reading I: Acts 5:17–26
Gospel: John 3:16–21

Reflection

Sunday school children sometimes carefully copy John 3:16 in their very best script: "God so loved the world that he gave his only Son, so that everyone who believes in him might not perish but might have eternal life." Taking a walnut, they remove the meat, and insert the carefully folded verse. They glue the walnut back together, paint it gold, and adorn it with precious beads or bits of glass. They then have the Gospel in a nutshell.

God has given a great gift, but John the Gospel writer laments "that the light came into the world, but people preferred darkness to light." It must not be that way with those who seek the truth. The opening prayer for today's liturgy reminds us that God has "filled us with the hope of resurrection / by restoring" us to our "original dignity." We hear often of original sin; this prayer, made in the radiance of Easter light, points us to our original dignity. We continue to pray that "we who relive this mystery each year / come to share it in perpetual love."

Ours is a grand vision and a great hope. Our celebration of the paschal mystery day by day prompts us, rejoicing, to remember that "God did not send his Son into the world to condemn the world, / but that the world might be saved through him."

Prayer

> Lord God,
> giver of all gifts,
> teach us to seek your light,
> to follow your way,
> to embrace your truth,
> that Christ may find a home in us
> and make our hearts to conform to his,
> for he lives and reigns with you
> and the Holy Spirit,
> one God, forever and ever.

When I am knocked off my horse

Reading I: Acts 9:1–20
Psalm: Psalm 117:1bc, 2
Gospel: John 6:52–59

Reflection
If you lined up one hundred Christians and asked them to write down what happened to Paul on the road to Damascus, 99.44 percent would be likely to write that he was knocked off his horse. Visitors to the magnificent Church of St. Paul the Apostle near Columbus Circle in New York City see an impressive frieze over the door depicting Paul falling toward Columbus Avenue with his horse.

But the Acts of the Apostles tells us: "On his journey, as he was nearing Damascus, a light from the sky suddenly flashed around him. He fell to the ground…" No horse. Where'd the horse story come from? Who knows, but it is ancient. But more important than the horse is that Paul "heard a voice saying to him, 'Saul, Saul, why are you persecuting me?' He said, 'Who are you, sir?' The reply came, 'I am Jesus, whom you are persecuting.'"

And at that moment was born not just Paul's theology of the Body of Christ, but perhaps even theology itself. For theology is faith seeking understanding. Paul, knocked down and blinded by the radiance of God's own Word, thinks that he has been persecuting the pesky sect of Jews for Jesus who were complicating life in the synagogue. Here it is revealed by the voice of God that it is the very Body of Christ that Paul persecutes.

When "things like scales fell from his eyes," Paul "regained his sight. He got up and was baptized, and when he had eaten, he recovered his strength."

We, as did Paul, eat to recover our strength. We, the Body of Christ, come to the eucharistic table that we might become more perfectly that which we already are: the Body of Christ. And we rejoice to hear the voice of Jesus promise in John's Gospel: "Whoever eats my flesh and drinks my blood remains in me and I in him. Just as the living Father sent me and I have life because of the Father, so also the one who feeds on me will have life because of me."

Prayer

> Almighty God,
> defender of the defenseless
> and refuge of the forlorn,

take pity on those who suffer,
and strengthen our hearts and our wills
that we may recognize your promise
and persevere in hope
even when darkness has fallen.
Console us with morning light
and the bright promise of the resurrection
through Christ our Lord.

God hugs you.
You are encircled by the arms
of the mystery of God.

• Hildegard of Bingen, 1098–1179

And so, in the end, what's the last word?

"Rejoice in the Lord always" (Phil 4:4a).

What was that?

"I shall say it again: rejoice" (Phil 4:4b).